SIMBAHÁN

An Illustrated Guide to 50 of the Philippines' Must-Visit Catholic Churches

REGALADO TROTA JOSÉ

Illustrated by ARCHITECT ALLAN JAY QUESADA

Simbahán: An Illustrated Guide to 50 of the Philippines' Must-Visit Catholic Churches

The Crown Book Group, Inc.
www.thecrownbookgroup.com

First published in the Philippines in 2020 by RPD Publications
a division of The Crown Book Group, Inc.

RPD Publications

Makati City Office
20/F, Zuellig Building,
Makati Avenue corner Paseo de Roxas,
Barangay Urdaneta, Makati City, 1225,
Metro Manila, Philippines

Quezon City Office
Unit 304, Marius Acropoli Building,
140 Katipunan Avenue, Barangay Saint Ignatius,
Quezon City, 1110, Metro Manila, Philippines

E-mail: info@rpdpublications.com
Website: www.rpdpublications.com

RPD Publications and the RPD Publications' colophon are registered
trademarks of The Crown Book Group, Inc.

Text Copyright © Regalado Trota José, 2020
Illustration Copyright © RPD Publications, 2020

ISBN: 978-621-8199-04-0

A CIP catalogue record for this book is available
from the National Library of the Philippines.

Printed in Singapore

Copy Editor: Ana B. Urbina
Layout & Design: Ana Angelica Gray
Author & Illustrator Digital Portraits: Earvin Renzo B. Basilio

From the author

Lovingly dedicated to the memory of my parents, Regalado San Luis José and Remedios Trota José, co-visitors to so many churches; and to all the heroic martyrs of the Covid-19 pandemic, who lived out the values of the churches the virus shut in vain.

From the illustrator

Lovingly dedicated to my grandparents, Alejandria Quesada and Soledad Altares, to my parents, Laureano Quesada and Jocelyn Quesada, and to my sister, Lauralyn Sumagaysay, who are all my foundation guides on Catholic faith; and to all the passionate servants of the Catholic church that keep the houses and foundation of our devotion standing still.

From the publishers

Lovingly dedicated to Theodore Louis Gray who is a living testament to the grace of the Black Nazarene and to the memory of the late R.P.D.

TABLE OF CONTENTS

INTRODUCTION

VISITING A *SIMBAHÁN*

While temples and stupas may be the architectural icons of much of Asia, the church is arguably the Philippines' most distinctive building. Through three hundred and fifty years of Hispanic rule, the indigenous names for places of worship were retained, instead of the Spanish *iglesia*. The word for "church" in much of central and southern Philippines, *simbahán*—accented on the final syllable—was chosen for this book's title, a conscious move away from the Manila way of naming things (which accents *simbahan* on the middle syllable). The word itself developed from *sambá*, to worship.

This guide, *Simbahán*, introduces fifty sites chosen among the country's most culturally or esthetically significant churches. Some were selected for their architectural significance, others for their well-preserved ornateness, still others for their picturesque settings. *Simbahán* points to areas otherwise not within the purview of the usual visitor: not just the far and the unheard-of, but also the very near or where there is art "not meant to be seen."

The formal building of churches began in 1565 with the coming of the Augustinians (known by their initials O.S.A.). One by one, the islands were enriched with religious edifices built under the aegis of the Franciscans (O.F.M.; they arrived in 1578), the Jesuits (S.J., 1581), the Dominicans (O.P., 1587), and the Augustinian Recollects (O.A.R., 1606). The Seculars, or diocesan priests subject to the bishop of a diocese, became involved in church building towards the end of the eighteenth-century; most of them were native Filipinos. With the end of Spanish rule in 1898, new religious orders arrived, each contributing to the church architectural heritage where they were assigned. Most were popularly known according to their place of origin: the Irish Fathers or Redemptorists (C.Ss.R., 1906), the Belgian Fathers (C.I.C.M., 1907), the Mill Hill Fathers (M.H.M., named after their mother house in London, 1908), and the German Fathers (S.V.D., 1909).

A typical church complex consisted of the church itself, a belltower on one side and the *convento* or rectory on the other, all fronting a wide plaza. Inside the church, the eye was led to the sanctuary at the end of the nave. Combining visual, didactic, and ritual importance was the *retablo*, an often elaborate altarpiece in front of which mass or other sacraments were celebrated.

The first buildings of wood, bamboo and thatch were eventually replaced by sturdier ones of stone and brick, and tile. Local climatic and geologic conditions tempered the height, width, and silhouette of constructions. A popular material was adobe, cut from volcanic tuff quarries, and quite distinct from its Latin American namesake of blocks formed from dried mud and straw. Layers of lime plaster or *palitada* protected walls from weathering. *Palitada* was also applied over *tabique pampango*, thin upper walls made of interwoven bamboo slats or split mangrove wood. Portland cement and galvanized iron sheets arrived in the late 19th century. Well into the 20th century, however, many structures still combined both wooden pillars and planks (just as in the native house) with masonry.

The designs for the churches and their decorations were drawn up not only by the priests and their assistants, but by military engineers, and Chinese and local *maestros de obras* (foremen). Professional architects only arrived in the second half of the 19th century. Construction teams were formed from those who paid their tribute in labor. Archival records inform us that they were fed and supplied with cigars. Women who helped in bringing sand and stones to the site were given iron needles. A town's importance was manifest in the size of its church buildings and the amount of worked silver mounted over the altars on fiestas.

Due to the vagaries of history and nature, one might encounter a church with a beautiful façade but be surprised with a less than complementary interior. Perhaps it was bombed in a war or unroofed in a storm. A well-conserved interior might be enclosed with a less-than-exceptional frontage. "Don't judge a church by its façade," one should be advised.

Nevertheless, each selection here effuses some facet of that cultural fusion of art, life and nature that could only blossom in the Philippines.

The recovery of the "authenticity" of these churches is an ongoing task, enmeshing contributions from anthropology, archaeology, architecture, archivistics, botany, chemistry, engineering, geography, history (with its various specializations), iconography, jurisprudence, linguistics, paleography, theology—the list grows longer as the study is refined. On hindsight, knowledge of these fields in some measure must have been utilized by the church builders. Hopefully, significances and recognition will turn up just in time before retablos are over-gilded, façades defaced, interiors over-baroque'd, images replaced with fakes, "decrepit" buildings demolished, or false information accepted as true.

In the present guidebook, the churches are divided into ten sections that correspond to geographic areas of the Philippines, running from north to south. Each visit begins with an introduction to the culture in which the church was built. Aspects of the façade and exterior are pointed out. Inside, the visitor is led to the sanctuary area, and from there the tour continues to the rest of the edifice or complex.

As this unabashedly Roman Catholic country celebrates 500 years of Christianity, *Simbahán* hopes to provoke a "wander-lust" among pilgrims and tourists—beyond the beaches and "fun"—to visit 50 remarkable monuments to the Filipinos' piety and artistry.

May your visit to a *simbahán* be spiritually nourishing. And do please come back, and visit more churches—whether *simbahán* or *simbahan*.

Regalado Trota José

Bell, *Soy la voz de Dios* (I am the voice of God)
Parish Church of Saint Mónica, Pan-ay, Capiz

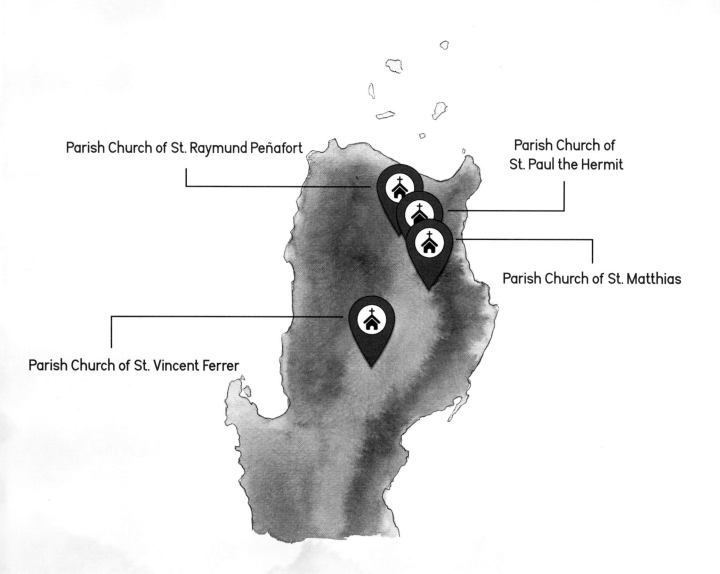

Parish Church of St. Charles Borromeo

Parish Church of St. Raymund Peñafort

Parish Church of
St. Paul the Hermit

Parish Church of St. Matthias

Parish Church of St. Vincent Ferrer

SECTION ONE: NORTHEASTERN LUZON

The northeastern side of Luzon, together with the offshore islands, was the sphere of the Dominican apostolate. Commencing in 1595 at Pata (now Namuac, Sanchez Mira), the friars reached out to the Babuyanes (1619) and Batanes (1783), and throughout the Cagayan River.

Towards the end of the 19th century, missions were established in Ifugao, which at that time formed part of Cagayan: Banaue under the Augustinians, and Kiangan under the Dominicans.

The Seculars took over in the 20th century, aided by the Belgian Fathers (C.I.C.M.) in 1908 in Nueva Vizcaya, and the German Fathers (S.V.D.), in northeastern Cagayan in 1933.

Parish Church of St. Charles Borromeo

Mahatao, Batan Island, 3901
Batanes, Philippines
Feast day: November 4
Prelature of Batanes

Mahatao is one of the handful of municipalities in Batanes, the northernmost province of the Philippines. A bit further north are islands that belong to the Republic of China (Taiwan). In fact certain ancient cultural traits like burials of bones in jars and a type of pendant called the *ling-ling-o* are shared with this storm-lashed region.

The Dominicans made a short visit to the area in 1686, but evangelization in earnest began in 1783, with a base in Basay, now Basco.

Mahatao was developed as a town in 1785, with streets laid at right angles. Masons from Luzon assisted in erecting the rip-rap buildings we see today.

Mahatao was separated from Basco and made an independent parish in the provincial chapter of the Dominicans in 1798. Soon after, a church and convento were built of stone, which lasted until a typhoon destroyed them in 1872. The parish was placed under the patronage of San Carlos Borromeo, a bishop who pioneered education during the Counter-Reformation (but also with a nod to the reigning monarch in Madrid, Carlos IV).

Father Crescencio Polo, parish priest from 1871 to 1883, built the present structures. The patron saint's symbols are featured below the belfry. One bell is dated 1874.

Rising above the façade is the *espadaña*, a free-standing belfry (José Rizal may have been inspired by this wall with holes to create Doña Victorina *de* de Espadaña, a crude social-climber).

The mid-19th century *beaterio*, with its tile roof still intact

In the main retablo, San Carlos Borromeo officiates from the central niche. To his sides are San José and Santa Catalina de Siena, and above him is Santo Domingo de Guzman, founder of the Order which built this church. The windows look like they were squeezed in between the massive buttresses.

The convento is unusual for its open porch that runs the length of the building, instead of being enclosed like the cantilevered balconies of colonial edifices. On one corner of the church yard is a brick-roofed *beaterio*. It was built in the middle of the 19th century to house a community of unmarried women who assisted the parish in maintaining the church, and in teaching the natives to read and write.

To the left of the church façade is a pillar meant to aid boatmen enter the narrow *vanuá* or port. Approaching from the sea, the navigator would fix his gaze on either of a pair of pillars nearer the beach and align it with the farther pillar.

C-scrolls in the upper flanges give a baroque touch to the mainly neoclassic central retablo.

Parish Church of St. Raymund Peñafort

Centro, Rizal (Malaueg), 3526
Cagayan, Philippines
Feast day: January 23
Archdiocese of Tuguegarao

Upon the request of a chief called Pagulayan, Dominicans accepted the spiritual administration of his village Malaueg (now known as Rizal) in 1608. A wooden church had already been built by then. Baptized Luis Pagulayan, the chief and his sister Luisa Ballinan led the people in improving its construction and decoration.

The town was the farthest inland from Lal-lo, the capital of the entire northeastern quadrant of Luzon. The Dominicans, hungry for the salvation of souls, looked forward to setting up a "base camp" here from where they could foray into the mountain fastnesses. And so, one auspicious November day in 1617, not only the bishop but the head of all the Dominicans in this part of Asia trudged all the way here to lay the first stone of the church. Slightly damaged by an earthquake in 1618, it was the largest church in the province west of the Cagayan River by about 1640 (it remains so today).

The date 1651 could originally be read on the façade of the rubble-work church of Malaueg (now Rizal), marking its rehabilitation after a fire.

Stairway leading from the inner courtyard to the 17th century convento

Ironically, the population of the hoped-for "showcase" settlement had decreased. Due to a fire in 1641 and the reduced number of churchgoers, a smaller apse was inserted into the original one. The renovation was finished in 1651. The later walls can be seen from the crumbling earlier apse of the left side of the church.

Both church and convento are almost wholly built of oval river stones, with a minimum of cut stone and brick. In the monument in front of the church are embedded blue and white and celadon plates dating from the late 16th or early 17th centuries, confirming the age of the constructions.

In the central niche of the central retablo is San Raymundo Peñafort, raising the cloak on which he sailed across the Mediterranean. He is the patron of canon lawyers.

The name Malaueg they say was formed from the river Matalág that flowed at the bottom of the hill, and *ueg*, the local word for river. Rizal/Malaueg has the distinction of hosting one of the earliest stone complexes in the country. Which adds to the irony of its ancient and unique name being replaced by another and newer one which is found nationally!

The central retablo is a composite of remnants of the 17th-18th century baroque original.

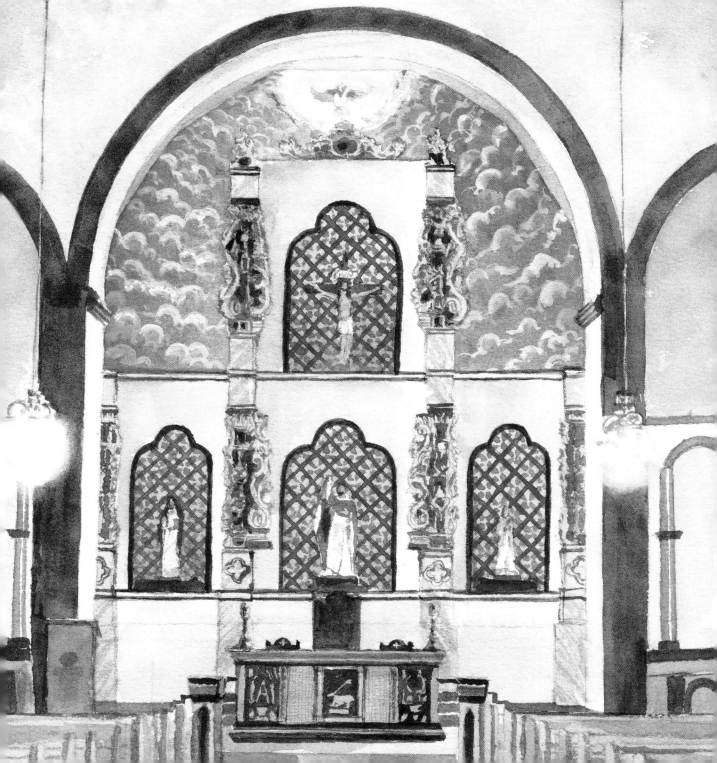

Parish Church of St. Paul the Hermit

National Highway, Población, San Pablo,
3329 Isabela, Philippines
Feast day: January 15
Diocese of Ilagan

Today's San Pablo was established in 1598 by the Dominicans, who tried to attract the Gaddang on the left of the Cagayan River and the Irraya on the right to settle here. In 1646 the present site was founded as a town and named Cabagan (possibly from *cabbagang*, a traveler). It was ecclesiastically accepted in 1647, under the patronage of San Pablo Apostol. The town was the most populous this side of the Valley, which is why the church is second only to Tuguegarao in size. A stone edifice in the 1650s collapsed in the earthquake of 1688. It was rehabilitated in the 1720s and made narrower, due to a diminishing population.

The façade and bell tower are of cut stone, and carved with graceful S-scrolls, twisted columns, volutes and bouquets that are typical of the 18th century. An old photograph in Madrid's Anthropology Museum may help in recovering the full majesty of this enigmatic frontage.

Political shifts in the late 19th century led to a split of the old town, with the original site eventually renamed San Pablo (rededicated to St Paul the Hermit) and two new towns baptized Cabagan (retaining the original patron, St Paul the Apostle) and Santa María respectively. The forgotten, sleepy aspect of San Pablo, the oldest Christian town in Isabela, is a stark contrast with the busy and brisk commerce at Cabagan, just a few kilometers away.

Though the façade and tower of San Pablo were probably early 1800s rehabilitations, both feature antiquated baroque motifs. The stone fence around the spacious atrium is ornamented with brick insets in which the name Domingo Babaran and the year 1813 may be barely read.

Bouquet-footed façade pilaster

Half of the nave is roofless, and is dominated by an imposing arch that used to support the choir loft. The walls this time are of brick, their courses interrupted by stone blocks and walled-up openings. The other half that is roofed houses the church proper. A chapel to the right used to lead to the old graveyard.

One is then faced with a cavernous brick vault, possibly that erected in the 1720s. What is now the transept is the original width of the three-naved 1650s stone church. The break between the 1650s construction and the 1720s narrowing can be discerned just before the middle of the present nave. The carved stones in the retablos flanking the sanctuary carry rococo motifs of the late 18th century; but they are weathered and seem to have been re-assembled rather loosely here from an unknown earlier location.

Just outside the town by the main road is the cemetery, built around the ruins of the brick chapel of San Vicente Ferrer. This was possibly built around 1724 as a vanguard to the town after a revolt.

In the massive sanctuary used to stand a *molave* retablo installed in 1804.

SECTION ONE: Northeastern Luzon

Parish Church of St. Matthias

**Maharlika Highway, Tumauini,
3325 Isabela, Philippines
Feast day: May 14
Diocese of Ilagan**

A chapel dedicated to San Matías de Tumauini was established in 1707 as a stopover for missionaries along the winding Cagayan River. A colony of wasps on the chapel's façade scared off the local Gaddangs and Irrayas, and the mission languished for a while. The town was founded in 1751, and what was to be the parish was established by the Dominicans in 1753. Official permission to build a permanent church was only given in 1783.

Under the direction of Father Domingo Fortó, son of a Catalan engineer, kilns to bake bricks were set up on the site of today's West Central School. He was assisted by a master mason named Castillejos from Lal-lo, the capital further north and by his confreres who shared their expertise. (Brick walls of the churches built by the Dominicans throughout Cagayan, even without the lime plaster protection, are more durable than those in Ilocos.)

The resulting complex at Tumauini represents the height of brick artistry in the Philippines. Terra cotta insets shaped as flowers, leaves, cornucopias, shells, suns, hearts, angels, and saints festoon all spaces inside and outside the church, the belltower, and even the serpentine-like fence. Some are even signed! Parts were numbered and marked to indicate their assembly into sinewy S-scrolls and leafy capitals.

Bricks inscribed with dates from 1783 to 1788 document the building of the church of Tumauini. The wedding-cake-like belltower was completed just after 1805.

Scroll with numbered bricks

The sanctuary is a gigantic scallop canopy flanked by oval windows and curved (instead of right-angled) corners.

Although the convento is mostly in ruins, there are stunning survivals: a vaulted ceiling over what is now a meeting hall, and impressive brickwork forming the interior of the chimney in the kitchen.

The round plan of the belltower is unique, found in only three other places in the Philippines. Like a wedding cake, brick insets contrast starkly with the whitewash. The largest bell was comissioned by Fortó as his "vocal" legacy when he left his beloved Tumauini in 1789 (after 19 long years) for a new assignment.

When Allied forces were flushing out Japanese forces in Cagayan (they were misdirected: the enemies were in Ifugao), residents trustingly stored their pianos in the church. Since the bombing in 1945, musical life in Tumauini has not been the same. Typhoons and good-intentioned but ill-fitting interventions are only some of the challenges that face Tumauini church. Tourists are advised to please avoid the temptation to pick up a decorated brick.

The interior was formerly white-washed, with red brick details.

Parish Church of St. Vincent Ferrer

Aritao-Quirino Road, Brgy. Dopaj, Dupax Del Sur,
3707 Nueva Vizcaya, Philippines
Feast day: April 5
Diocese of Bayombong

The parish church of San Vicente Ferrer is nestled in a peaceful valley in Dupax del Sur. The town's name is said to be taken from the archaic spelling of a local word meaning "to lie down on one's back." Though the local inhabitants called themselves Immeas, they became more popularly known as Isinay. Augustinian pioneers settled five villages here in 1722. When the Dominicans formally took over in 1741, they complemented the fruit trees and irrigated rice fields with orchards, gardens of cacao and mongo, and cattle-filled corrals.

After a wooden church burned down in 1755 and again in 1766, Father Manuel Corripio—who would be curate for 17 years (1769-1786)—made plans to erect one of brick. With the collaboration of the leaders Salirungan and Tordoya, the expertise of masons and workers from Tuguegarao church (whose distinct silhouette from 1766 was copied here), and the assistance of the women (who carried clay and sand for the masonry)—and the earnings from cacao—work began in 1774.

The church was functional in two years' time: a brick over the doorway is marked 1776. Completed in 1782, this was to be the first and oldest masonry church—in the oldest existing pueblo founded by the Spaniards—in Nueva Vizcaya. The project paved the way for the construction of brick churches in nearby Aritao, Bambang, and Bayombong, all in the last two decades of the 18th century.

The church in Dupax del Sur was built in 1774 to 1782. The convento was finished in 1778, while the bell-tower was constructed in stages: 1775, 1776, 1786, then 1788.

Richly carved choir loft pillar

The gems of the church are the elaborate carvings on sandstone that enliven the twin pillars that support the choir loft, and the walls of the baptistry. In this claustrophobic room, where every inch is a translation of the baroque into the indigene, a waving Christ figure welcomes visitors. In front of the sanctuary is the tombstone of Father Antonio Xabet, who lovingly ministered here for 41 years in the 19th century. He also erected the ponderous "flagpole" in front of the church yard.

In 1898, the Dominicans left Dupax also with a tribunal, two schools, and bridges, all of brick. For almost the next century, the parish was under the care of the Congregation of the Immaculate Heart of Mary or "Belgian Fathers," until it was turned over to the Diocese of Bayombong.

Baroque parts from the earlier 18th century altarpiece were reassembled for the central retablo.

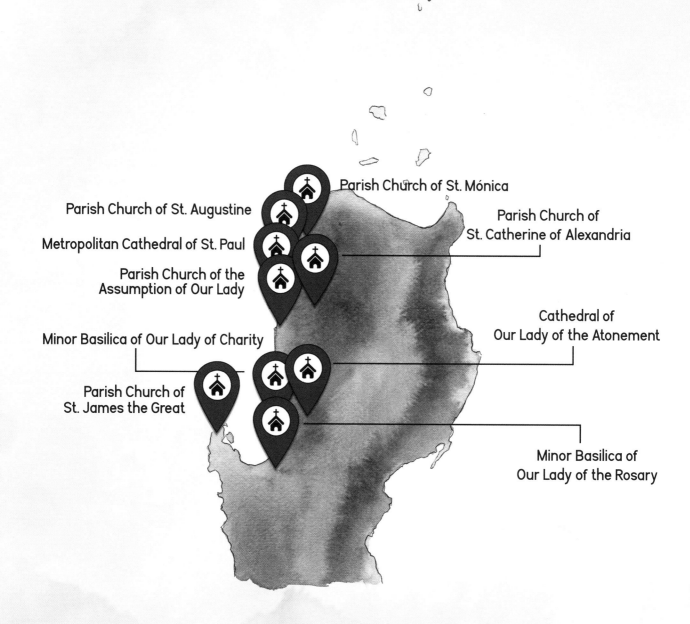

Parish Church of St. Mónica

Parish Church of St. Augustine

Parish Church of
St. Catherine of Alexandria

Metropolitan Cathedral of St. Paul

Parish Church of the
Assumption of Our Lady

Cathedral of
Our Lady of the Atonement

Minor Basilica of Our Lady of Charity

Parish Church of
St. James the Great

Minor Basilica of
Our Lady of the Rosary

SECTION TWO: NORTHWESTERN LUZON

The entire Ilocos region was Christianized by the Augustinians, beginning in 1586 at Bauang, Tagudin, Laoag, and Batac. In the Cordillera, the first church was probably erected in Kayan (now in Tadian, Mountain Province), about 1667. After Vigan became a cathedral in 1758, the Seculars built churches in the environs.

The Dominicans labored in central and western Pangasinan, commencing in 1587 at Binalatongan (now San Carlos City), and briefly in La Union (1772-1790). The Augustinian Recollects began their apostolate in Zambales (present-day eastern Pangasinan) in 1609 at Bolinao.

In the 20th century, congregations from Germany and Belgium assumed many of these ministries together with the Seculars.

Parish Church of St. Mónica

Brgy. 6 San Leandro, Población, Sarrat, 2914
Ilocos Norte, Philippines
Feast day: May 4
Diocese of Laoag

Under the Augustinians, the mission of San Miguel de Sarrat was made independent of Laoag in 1724. In 1807 the *cailianes* (townsfolk) rose up in arms against government control of local *basi* wine, and again in 1815 against the fraudulent transactions of the *principales* or local elite. In this last uprising Rosa Agcaoili, the priest's housekeeper who undervalued *inabel* woven goods, was killed and a certain body part was sliced, dried, and nailed to the church doors. The enraged *cailianes* sacked the houses and drank the church wine. Government troops retook the town, only to have it burned. Incidents such as these led to the halving of the Ilocos into two provinces in 1818. Sarrat, of all places, was the initial capital of Ilocos Norte; but this title was given to Laoag within the year.

Sarrat moved to its present location, not far from its ruins. The church buildings constructed of brick in the 1830s suffered a fire in 1882, but were grandly rebuilt in the 1890s. The tower and convento, like others in the Ilocos, were built away from the nave to minimize damage during a tremor. Earthquakes especially that of 1983 significantly modified both tower and façade.

The façade sported a pediment similar to other 19th century neoclassic churches in Ilocos, although this was greatly altered after the earthquake of 1983. The arch on the right is one of three that form a unique bridge linking the church to the convent.

Rare example of trusswork

The church at 105 meters is the longest in Ilocos Norte. The complex double system of rafters and trusses (a whole forest!) is an engineering marvel. The pieces are so fixed to each other that there is no need for pillars to hold them up. Although this trusswork is the kind that was used all over the country during the Spanish era, only an exceedingly precious few are left; these must be studied for their insights on Philippine technology. One of the last surviving examples was taken down from a cathedral in dubious circumstances.

A bridge on three domes links the church with the convento. The brick work over the domes allows a whisper from one corner to be picked up on the opposite corner. Both floors of the sprawling convento are of brick, which is also characteristic of the region. The solid walls of the second floor shield the inner brick walls from the heat, like a thermos. Only about half of the building is lived in, the rest is exposed to the elements. Some of the ruins are so dramatic that excitable minds imagine a guillotine room, when in fact the French instrument never reached these shores.

The staid neoclassicism of the central retablo is relieved by floral details sprouting from the flanges and niche frames.

Parish Church of St. Augustine

Bgy. Veronica, Paoay, 2902
Ilocos Norte, Philippines
Feast day: May 5
Diocese of Laoag

According to a story, Paoay originated in a place called Callaguip (Ilocano for "to remember"). Coralstone boulders pried from the sand dunes here were floated down the river to the present site. They were prepared for the church which the Augustinians had commenced towards the end of the 17th century. The bulk of the edifice was up by the early 18th century, but earthquakes and typhoons necessitated continuous renovations. Witnesses to all these vicissitudes are the shifts in construction materials. In the façade, the lower section is of brick, the upper of irregularly cut stone. In the rear, the order is reversed. Income from the town's weavers of blankets and sails contributed largely to the project, unquestionably the icon for Philippine baroque.

The best time to appreciate the façade is about an hour before sunset. It turns golden! The details come into relief: the languorous coiled fern left of the entrance, the sun and moon flanking the image of San Agustín, and above it the Spanish coat-of-arms, with remains of Chinese lions poised on either side.

The hulking squatness of the church—with its uneven plastered rough stone-and-brick masonry—contrasts with the upright erectness, barefaced and finely-fitted cut stone of the belltower to its left.

Begun in the last years of the 17th century, the bulk of Paoay's church of rubblework and brick was standing by the early 18th century. The belltower of cut coralstone is dated 1793.

More preserved details on the left side entrance

Twenty-four humongous buttresses with volute tracings (like *sampaguita* blooms on wrestlers' biceps) bolster the church like a phalanx. The pair that flank the façade have double volutes. Two others are stairways that enabled workers to fix the roof, which being blown off so many times accounts for the relative bareness of the interior.

The last Augustinian, Baldomero Real, updated the decrepit church. Stoic pilasters were imposed over the wide-arched entrances. Paired Doric columns lifted the choir loft (now non-existent) and marked the nave from the sanctuary. (The trademark twin columns support the municipal hall a block away—also one of Real's projects.) Roman temple-like retablos were positioned over windows, so their bulkiness was mollified by the light-suffused niches. The new look was inaugurated on his birthday in 1896, but he had to leave it all—painted ceiling, glass windows, and especially an elegant wrought-iron pulpit emblazoned with his initials ("B.R." was after all chief homilist at San Agustín in Manila)—in 1898.

To see samples of the textiles that built Paoay, visit the Museo Ilocos Norte beside the Provincial Capitol in Laoag.

The interior went through a thorough neoclassic make-over in the 1890s.

METROPOLITAN CATHEDRAL OF ST. PAUL

Burgos Street, Vigan City, 2700
Ilocos Sur, Philippines
Feast day: January 25
Archdiocese of Nueva Segovia

The seat of the diocese of Nueva Segovia which was founded in Cagayan in 1595 was relocated to more accessible Vigan, Ilocos Sur in 1758.

The city, also known as Ciudad Fernandina was named, they say, after the *biga* or taro plant. It overlooked the junction of the Govantes (then Buquid) and Mestizo Rivers, themselves branches of the great Abra River.

The first "Vigan" bishop died on the way to his see, but some of the silver vessels he commissioned are still assembled on the Holy Thursday Altar in the cathedral.

The present three-naved cathedral was begun in 1790 and inaugurated in 1797, but repaired several times. Blocks of coralstone make up the mass of the edifice; brick was added in subsequent extensions such as the sacristy and adjacent convento, apse, and upper walls. Perched on the façade's Doric frieze are diminutive Chinese lions. Frothy late 18th century rococo elements sprout around openings and frames.

The cathedral and belltower of Vigan, completed in 1797, were set-off by wide plazas to diminish the chances of catching fire from surrounding buildings. A second tower was planned to the left of the cathedral.

The interior is a mélange of the late 18th to early 19th century art. Left of the sanctuary is a retablo transiting between the rococo and the neoclassic. The one to the right, illustrating the mysteries of the rosary, is from the 1890s. The ceiling emulates a ribbed vault in wood, the way San Sebastian (Manila) does in metal.

The episcopal palace, known locally as the Palacio, was begun about 1783 and repaired several times. Built astride the Govantes (then Buquid) River, its occupants were afforded a good view of the waterway (and of any suspicious arrivals). Almost the entire second floor is composed of *capiz* windows, which hide an important ecclesiastical museum.

Chinese lion from the seminary, now at the Palacio

Across the Palacio, next to the belltower, stood the seminary which was opened in 1822. It allowed lay externs to study in the 1890s, and educated the region's clergy and influencers such as labor leader Isabelo de los Reyes and Father Gregorio Aglipay. It burned down in 1968, its ruins impiously encased later in pseudo-colonial fast food establishments.

On the far end of the plaza across the cathedral, the Holy Rosary College for girls was inaugurated in 1892. Formerly run by Dominican Sisters, the gracefully arcaded building is now a mall.

Vigan's cathedral complex (with the unfortunate exception of the old seminary grounds) is the most integral in the country. But that is hardly manifest in the current tourist hype and sputtering tricycles.

The principal retablo was commissioned in the 1840s by the parish priest, Estanislao Bumantay.

Parish Church of the Assumption of Our Lady

4 Burgos Road, Santa María, 2705
Ilocos Sur, Philippines
Feast day: August 15
Archdiocese of Nueva Segovia

The church complex of Santa María appears as a citadel, the Ilocano version of the Acropolis. As depicted on a wall next to the façade, the Virgin Mary is said to have repeatedly appeared on a guava tree on the present slipper-shaped hill.

The parish was founded in 1769 under the care of the Augustinians. The church built after this time was of rubblework, still visible in the bays between the humongous buttresses of brick. The same rough stone was used for the first level of the octagonal belltower, the solid walls covering all the sides of the hill, and the four sets of stairways communicating with the town. Three of the stairways are on the west side: the main one with 85 steps, a second beside the belltower, and the third behind the old convento. The fourth on the eastern side leads to the cemetery and beyond it, the mountain trails to Abra.

The late 18th century rubblework church of Santa María was rehabilitated with brick in the early 19th century. A bridge connected the choir loft to the convento in front of the church.

Entrance arch to the abandoned cemetery, east of the citadel

In 1822 Santa María became a jumping-off point for missionaries bound for the adjoining province of Abra. This explains the extraordinary number of retablos flanking the sanctuary, which permitted up to seven priests to simultaneously celebrate their own mass. A stairway behind the main altar provided direct access to the old convento adjoining the apse. Eventually a much larger residence to accommodate more missionaries was built facing the church, on the grounds that may have previously served as a place of refuge for the townspeople fleeing an attack. Gothic windows in the quarters behind attest to extensive renovation in the 1890s: this project (and presumably others like it) is said to have provoked many families to move south, eventually founding the town of Cuyapo, Nueva Ecija. Only ruins of a wall remain of the passage that connected the second level of the convento with the choir loft.

The rounded pediment of the church is echoed by the twin façades of the school on the western foot of the hill and the chapel of the cemetery at the end of the walkway on the east. It appears that the inner core of the church was stabilized by "sandwiching" it in brick (like in Majayjay, Laguna). The width of the nave was so reduced that the side retablos before the sanctuary are at a diagonal, and not at right angles with the walls. Of interest are two large baptismal fonts: one shallow, one like a tub (for older converts?).

The sanctuary's extra retablos were constructed after 1822 for the Abra missionaries.

Parish Church of St. Catherine of Alexandria

Tayum, 2803
Abra, Philippines
Feast day: November 25
Diocese of Bangued

In Tayum converged three rivers: the Abra, which led to Vigan in the west; the Lagben to Benguet in the south; and the Tineg to the northern heartland of the province, where Itneg was spoken. The Augustinians were the pioneer missionaries in Abra, but by the 18th century the district was administered by diocesan clergy assigned from Vigan. Under the direction of these mostly Ilocano priests, churches of brick and stone were built in Bangued (possibly late 18th century) and in nearby Tayum (about 1830). The Augustinians returned to Abra beginning in the 1840s, but the ministries of these two towns were turned over to them only in the 1890s. The Augustinians left in 1898; they were replaced in 1911 by priests of the Society of the Divine Word (S.V.D.), who labored here for many years. (The bishop of Vigan, Dennis Dougherty requested the Society's founder Arnold Janssen in 1909 to send missionaries to Abra.)

The baroque outline of the church façade is embraced by the kind of volutes that are seen in many Ilocos churches. Three cornices run across the façade but curiously the two upper levels are abbreviated before reaching the sides. Propping the volutes are rotund finials that recall *burnay* earthenware vessels. The first two levels of the belltower date from around 1869; old women recount their grandmothers carrying sand for its construction. In the upper levels of concrete are bells from France blessed in 1950.

Under the direction of Secular priests of Tayum, the church was built around 1830, while the lower two levels of the tower were constructed about 30 years later. The volutes give a baroque touch to the otherwise neoclassic façade.

Local interpretation of Western motifs on the baptismal font

Finials similar to those on the façade accent the neoclassic retablos, which are enlivened by vegetal details (possibly even leaves of the *tayum* indigo plant). The pedestals supporting images in the niches of the side retablos look like sheaves of grain, but they also recall the tight-waisted wooden mortars where rice is pounded. A polychromed hardwood baptismal font with ebullient carvings of leaves and fruit is an important example of local art.

After the convento was burned in 1891, the parish priest acquired a house just across the church from the plaza that belonged to Capitán Raymundo Cariño. When the Sisters Servants of the Holy Spirit (S.Sp.S.) settled here in 1912, the priests moved to a new *tagnawa* (community-built) rectory next to the sacristy. Both the S.V.D. and the S.Sp.S. were founded by Janssen, who was canonized in 2003. From their cradle in Tayum, these two German-speaking congregations proceeded with their apostolic work to Manila (Holy Ghost College, 1913), Quezon City (Christ the King Seminary, 1934), and elsewhere.

The central retablo is an upland version of a neoclassic prototype.

MINOR BASILICA OF OUR LADY OF CHARITY

MacArthur Highway cor. Grotto Road, Agoo, 2504
La Union, Philippines
Feast day: May 4 (Parish of Santa Mónica)
Diocese of San Fernando de La Union

Agoo was known since the 1580s as the Port of Japan, where Japanese traders procured local products especially deer pelts (up to 80,000 annually). The Franciscans established a mission here in 1578 "by the river of the same name" (which probably derived from a local pine called *agoho* or *aroo*). Curiously, no river runs by Agoo at present; the port may have been at the river by Aringay close to the north, or at the estuary of Santo Tomas just to the south.

The Augustinians, taking over in 1598, dedicated the church to Santa Mónica, the mother of San Agustín. An earthquake in 1892 destroyed the church buildings; only the ground level of the belltower remained. Another earthquake in 1990 damaged the present church (1975-1978), designed in an eclectic style by Ignacio Palma Bautista, and repairs were inaugurated in 2001. However, the remnant of the old belltower collapsed under the weight of a massive concrete cross mounted on it.

The façade of the present church of Agoo alludes to the Franciscan founding of the town by incorporating elements from the California mission churches built by their confreres across the Pacific.

The church enshrines the wooden image of Our Lady of Charity, fondly called Apo Caridad ("Lady Charity") by the Ilocanos and countless other devotees who believe she has succored them in innumerable ways. Her right hand is stretched open, as if bestowing graces on those who call on her. Her tunic and blue mantle, which is slung over the left shoulder, differ in iconography from another famous Apo Caridad, venerated in Bantay, Ilocos Sur. This latter image is attired in a regal gown, with a cape over her shoulders. The belt or *correa* of the Augustinians (who evangelized the entire Ilocos region) hangs conspicuously from her waist. In recognition of the people's ancient devotions, both miraculous images were canonically crowned: Bantay's Apo Caridad in 1956, and Agoo's in 1971.

Our Lady of Charity is enthroned in the high altar of the church in Agoo, which was declared a minor basilica in 1982. Within the church complex are various interesting works of art. Near the entrance is "The Second Coming of Christ," painted by Rey Gimeno. The artist included a number of recognizable personalities from a previous era. In the garden is a bell dated 1815 and dedicated to Santa Mónica; it was stolen but happily recovered from Bugallon, Pangasinan, in 1963. The museum, dedicated to two native sons who became bishops, exhibits sculptures by Mariano Aspiras Madriaga, first archbishop of Lingayen-Dagupan, and memorabilia of Antonio Ll. Mabutas, first bishop of Laoag.

The central baldaquin is reminiscent of those in Roman basilicas.

Kararag Ken Apo Caridad

O nasam-it unay a Virgen Maria, nadungo unay a katalekmi, Nuestra Señora de la Caridad,
kinayatmo O Señora ti naisaad iti tronom iti dayta napateg a santuaryo,
tapno makitam, mapaliiwmo dagiti adu a rigrigatmi ken mapardasan ti umarayat kadakami,
ken tapno dakam amin nga anakmo iti amin nga il-ili itanggadmi kenka dagiti umas-asug a matami.
Idalannakami a nakaay-ay-ay nga anakmo; iturongnakami a sumbrek iti santuaryom
ken umasideg nga agdawat iti tulong ken pannarawidwidmo.

O Ina, dinakam kad baybay-an;
isalakannakam iti sulisog, iti bisin, iti kiddit ti tudo,
saksakit, dakes a pammatulad, ken balikug a pannursuro.
Timudem dagiti sasainnekmi; kaasiannakam kadagiti pakaeigatanmi ditoy a biag.
Ket, Apo, igun-odannakam kadagiti naruay a grasiam tapno maragpatmi met koma ti biag nga agnanayon. Amen.

Excerpt from *Nobena kenni Nuestra Señora de Caridad de Agoo*
Minor Basilica of Our Lady of Charity, Agoo, La Union, 2020

Prayer to Our Lady of Charity

Oh, most gracious Virgin Mary, Our most loving and dependable Lady of Charity,
You wished to be enthroned in the precious sanctuary,
where you can see and feel our many sufferings, and then quickly come to our aid,
therefore, all of us will turn our tear-filled eyes to you.
Guide us through the right path, and lead us to your sanctuary
so we can bring our pleas for help and guidance to you.

Oh Mother, do not abandon us;
deliver us from temptation, famine, drought, evil examples, and false teachings.
Hear our supplications, have mercy on our daily needs.
Dear Lady, obtain for us your bountiful graces so that we may attain eternal life. Amen.

Image of Our Lady of Charity, canonically crowned in 1971

CATHEDRAL OF OUR LADY OF THE ATONEMENT

Mt. Mary Hill, Cathedral Loop, Baguio City, 2600
Benguet, Philippines
Feast day: July 9
Diocese of Baguio

Baguio appears in records as early as 1854 as a village of La Trinidad, the capital of Benguet province. It took its name from *bagyu*, an Ibaloi term for a common swamp fern. The development of Baguio in the early 1900s as the gateway to the potentials of the Cordillera (particularly the cool climate, and the gold mines) led to the call for missionaries by the bishop of Vigan. The prelate assigned the first three members of the Congregation of the Immaculate Heart of Mary (C.I.C.M., or the Belgian Fathers) to Baguio in 1907; shave their beards first, he advised them. A house in the middle of Session Road, the main street, was converted into a chapel dedicated to Saint Patrick and a school for boys (from which originated today's University dedicated to Saint Aloysius Gonzaga).

In 1919 a larger church of concrete was begun atop the hill a short climb above the compound. The project was spearheaded by Father Florimund Carlu, according to the design of Father Leon Vendelmans with the assistance of Father Adolph Cansse (both were civil engineers). In 1924 the church still lacked its twin towers, but mass could be said in 1933. It was finally consecrated in 1936, and dedicated to Our Lady of the Atonement in honor of the devotion of the Franciscans in Graymoor, New York, who generously supported its construction. Its soaring silhouette is Gothic, but the details are Romanesque.

Baguio Cathedral was built in the 1930's due to the efforts of Belgian missionaries, American sponsors, Japanese carpenters, and Ibaloi and Ifugao craftsmen.

Fish-tailed rooster weathervane

The bronze crucifix on the main altar is said to have been worked from a bag of coins donated by an old Ibaloi woman (the original has been replaced for safekeeping). Much of the woodwork, including the main altar, was the handiwork of the Japanese master carpenter Teruji Okubo. Under his supervision, students of the Saint Louis Trade School assembled the seasoned pinewood pews. The panels of saints surrounding the semicircular chancel, and other pieces were carved by a man from Hapao, Ifugao, named Alberto or Obool. The stained-glass windows crafted by the Kraut company in Manila were donated by local families. The bells were cast in 1932 in Louvain, Belgium. An image of Saint Patrick keeps watch on the right covered walk.

The church earned the title of cathedral when the first prelate of the Apostolic Prefecture of Montañosa was installed in 1933. The Calvary on the atrium commemorates the victims of the bombing at the end of World War II in 1945.

The decoration of the chancel and main altar has been kept low, to give prominence to the bright colors of the stained-glass windows.

Minor Basilica of Our Lady of the Rosary

Milo St., Población, Manaoag, 2430
Pangasinan, Philippines
Feast day: Oct. 7
Archdiocese of Lingayen-Dagupan

Thanks to the ever-expanding expressway system, it takes only about two and a half hours to reach Manaoag from Manila. The challenge, therefore, is to remain cool while negotiating a parking space and gently maneuvering through the crowds of pilgrims. But upon entering the church, whatever one's inconveniences in getting here vaporize with the lingering scent of incense from the previous mass. For there, on the high altar, is the image of Our Lady and her Son gazing placidly over the throng. We are told that centuries ago the Lady made a call (*taoag* in the Pangasinan language, hence this place's name) to a passing farmer, telling him from a treetop that she wanted a church to be built on this spot.

In 1605 the Dominicans accepted this mission from the Augustinians, and a chapel heeding the Lady's *taoag* was built. Not long after the installation of the image of Our Lady of the Rosary in the church, miracles began to take place. In 1627, a dead girl from Binmaley was brought back to life when laid by her parents at the feet of the Lady. In 1697, a fire in the sacristy was put out when the priest threatened to throw himself (and, rather unchivalrously, the image of Our Lady) into the blaze. Alleviation from plagues, droughts, and epidemics was attributed to Our Lady. The ancient image is of carved wood, with ivory additions.

The inner core of the church of Manaoag dates from the early 1700s, while the façade was renovated in the 1920s. The belltower is a 1954 replacement of another that cracked in the 1892 earthquake.

The inner core of the present brick church dates from 1701 to 1722. It was a donation by a pious couple, Gaspar de Gamboa and Agueda Yangta. They also built a chapel on the alleged first site of the town, by the cemetery across the Baloquing River. A transept was begun in 1882, but the effects of an earthquake in 1892 and a fire in 1898 (which destroyed more than two centuries' accumulation of gifts and records) are witnessed by the variously sized buttresses holding up the nave.

In 1909 a new set of altarpieces from the studio of Isabelo Tampinco was inaugurated. He was the foremost sculptor of the day. He incorporated the twisted columns of the early 1700s retablo in the side altars.

In 1960, local artist Francisco Zarate completed four murals on the walls of the transept depicting the first *taoag*, the miracles of 1627 and 1697, and the canonical coronation of Our Lady in 1926. Our Lady's shrine was declared a Minor Basilica in 2015.

The central retablo of 1909 is one rare documented altarpiece by Isabelo Tampinco.

Himno ed Pamalanget na Maglorian Virgen ed Manaoag Patrona ed Amianey Luzon (1926)

Coro:
Gloria gloriay itanila tayó, ed maligan Patronay Manaoag.
Cabalbaleyan, galin ontáoag, ed malágac a Ynay Dios tayó.

Estrofa 1a:
Dia'd amianey Luzón nibiig can manangiésel ed sáry irap mi.
dia'd Rosariom, Yná, asagmac mi'y panangarom a sancabalgán.
Cailoco-an tan Pangasinán mainán tólong mo so ibelbeliao.

capagno sicálay queneliao lápag mi'y tampol ya inosdongan
Dia'd Tarlac man no dia'd Cagayaán, dia'd Zambales tan Nueva Vizcaya,
say mataoen mon pananyampayu so laoas dan pantintindecán.

Coro: Gloria gloria itanila tayó, etc.

Estrofa 2a:
Canián natan mablin balanget so idacmomo min itoo'd Sicá.
Sicay arin bidbiren mi laya lapoay nagnap min liget.
Dia'd capalandeyan tan dia'd láoac, ilog may colós sobol no dayat,
Oley mo comoy laoas icayat tan mainán logor moy nioacáoac.
Sicá Yna, so Arin bidbiren mi, Virge'd Manaoag a sancablián.
Cayarián mi ray bendicionan; natan tan naani ilaban cami, natan tan naani ilaban cami.

Coro: Gloria gloria itanila tayó, etc.

- Lyrics: P. A. Bañez; Music: J. B. Bañez.
Archivo de la Universidad de Santo Tomás, Manila

Hymn for the canonical coronation of the glorious Virgin of Manaoag, patroness of Northern Luzon (1926)

Refrain: Glory, glory, we praise the joyous patroness of Manaoag.
Province-mates, come let us call on our generous Mother of God.

1. In Northern Luzon she is there to intercede for all our sufferings.
Through your rosary, Mother, we found your great love for us.
Throughout Ilocos and Pangasinan we proclaim your motherly assistance.
Whenever we call on you, you promptly hear our cries.
Whether in Tarlac, Cagayan, Zambales or Nueva Vizcaya,
your gentle, heavenly embrace is always felt.

Refrain: Glory, glory, we praise, etc.

2. And so today, we humbly lay on your head a precious crown.
We acknowledge you as our Queen, the source of our greatest joy.
Over the mountains, valleys, rivers or creeks, springs or seas,
We loudly proclaim your motherly care.
You, Mother, are our Queen, our dearest Virgin of Manaoag.
Bless all our concerns and needs; protect us now and forever, protect us now and forever.

Refrain: Glory, glory, we praise, etc.

Image of Our Lady of Manaoag, canonically crowned in 1926

PARISH CHURCH OF ST. JAMES THE GREAT

**Brgy. Germinal, Bolinao, 2406
Pangasinan, Philippines
Feast day: July 25
Diocese of Alaminos**

The port of Bolinao has received travelers for centuries, as witnessed by 14th century Chinese jars in nearby burial sites. The recent theory that Blessed Odoric of Pordenone said mass here in 1324 is doubted by most historians, since his itinerary is more logically linked to Borneo or Singapore.

During the Spanish era, the Christian community was under various religious administrations: the Augustinians (1584-1596), the Dominicans (1596-1600), the Augustinians (1600-1609), the Augustinians Recollects (1609-1679), the Dominicans (1679-1712), the Recollects (1712-1784), the Seculars (1784-1850), and back to the Recollects (1850-1898).

Early religious buildings were burned in 1623 and 1660. The royal seals of Spain on the present façades of both church and convento provide a construction clue. In the center of both seals is the escutcheon of the House of Bourbon-Anjou (three fleur-de-lis), which was added to the Spanish coat-of-arms in 1700. These buildings then were probably constructed during the 70-year period between the resumption of the Augustinian Recollects in Bolinao in 1712 and their departure in 1784. Eight-pointed stars over the second-level windows refer to the Recollects' patron in the Philippines, San Nicolás de Tolentino. The identification of two more seals on the church façade could narrow the dating.

Both church and convento are clad in cleanly squared coralstone. The trefoil arch over the church's main entrance is accented by unique, finely cut fleur-de-lis points.

The cut coralstone church of Bolinao was built sometime between 1712 and 1784. Bells dating from 1749 and 1793 hang from the belltower, which was damaged in 1788 and repaired later.

A crowned Oriental lion tackles a fantastic tree on this church door

The nave is stabilized by a pair of step-buttresses. Both sides of the interior are lined with galleries, added to accommodate the growing population. The three retablos and pulpit are in the neoclassic style, and one wonders what happened to the earlier pieces. A significant "left-over" is the baroque retablo, possibly early 18th century, in the baptistry. Tentative incisions on the smooth columns suggest that they were intended to bear more florid, twisted carving. Even more interesting are the monster-head pedestals of the retablo, which with their bulging eyes, bulbous nose and extended tongue resemble truss brackets in the conventos of Lóboc (Bohol) and Zamboanga.

Bolinao received the Venerable Madre Jerónima de la Asunción in 1612, on her way to found the monastery of Santa Clara in Manila. The next year, 1622, Bolinao saw the departure of the Augustinian Recollects Francisco de Jesús and Vincent de San Antonio for Nagasaki, where they were martyred. They were beatified in 1867.

The neoclassic retablo unusually resembles a pavilion meant for a Roman-style garden.

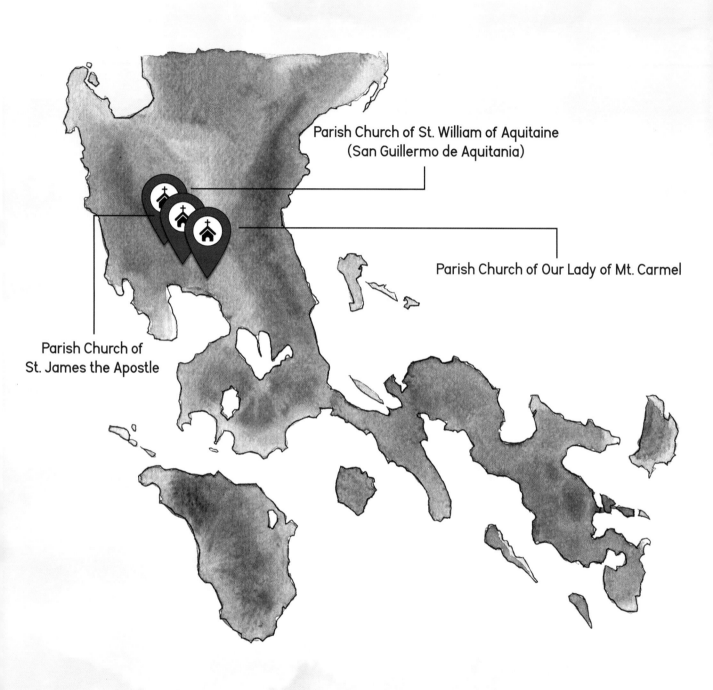

Parish Church of St. William of Aquitaine
(San Guillermo de Aquitania)

Parish Church of Our Lady of Mt. Carmel

Parish Church of
St. James the Apostle

SECTION THREE: CENTRAL LUZON

The pioneers in the central plain just north of Manila were the Augustinians, commencing in 1572 with Lubao and Betis in southern Pampanga, and Calumpit in present-day Bulacan province. The Franciscans began their southern Bulacan mission in Meycauayan (1578).

On the Bataan peninsula, the Dominicans initiated their work in Abucay (1587). On the western side of Bataan and north through Zambales, the Augustinian Recollects began with Mariveles, Subic and Masinloc (1607). All these Orders continued their work in the later provinces of Tarlac and Nueva Ecija. In 1771 Pampanga was assigned to the Seculars, who ministered up to 1860 in some parishes.

SECTION THREE: Central Luzon

Parish Church of St. James the Apostle

Betis, Guagua, 2003
Pampanga, Philippines
Feast days: July 25 and December 30
Archdiocese of San Fernando, Pampanga

The Augustinians established a mission in Betis in 1572 and formalized it in 1608. It was one of the first in Pampanga. The diocesan clergy took over Betis from 1771 to about 1810; the Augustinians continued until 1949.

Construction of the present edifice is supposed to have started in 1660, but repairs were still being carried out in the 1790s. A local tree called *betis* was said to have been so large that it supplied all the woodwork for the church. Cut adobe stone was used for most of the church; walls of adobe alternating with brick like a chessboard are found in the sacristy, belltower, and convento. The church had two belltowers.

Much of the church of Betis dates from the 18th century, although a second belfry was pulled down after the 1812 earthquake. The façade was redecorated in the 1920s.

Playful angel and guitar on the central retablo

The central retablo is a landmark in the art history of the country. It is joyously baroque with its gesticulating saints, twisted columns intertwined with garlands, angels playing instruments, and rarely seen *estípites* (inverted obelisks). In 1790, the altarpiece had been newly installed and had not even been painted yet. This dating jives with the rococo details over the frames and the panels at the base of the retablo. The overall white background with touches of gilding and polychrome is proper for the late 18th century. The retablo in the baptistry was possibly assembled from remnants of other 18th century altarpieces.

Another glory of the church is the painted ceiling, which dates from about the 1890s with later renovations. In the *Second Coming of Christ*, one can figure out a gentleman in a suit and a lady in a *terno* without the *pañuelo* neck scarf, which was fashionable in the 1920s-1930s. This section must have been timed with the inauguration in 1928 of the Sacred Heart of Jesus monument in front of the church. The "modernization" of the central section of the pediment of the façade also dates from this period. On the main doors is *Jacob's Dream* carved by Juan Flores, one of Betis' 20th century prolific artists.

Residents credit their patron Apung Tiago (St. James) with holding up the dike against the lahar flows from Mount Pinatubo in the mid-90's. During his fiesta, devotees dance the *kuraldal* which commemorates the saint's intervention over the enemy. On Easter Monday resident artisans honor Saint Joseph, patron of carpenters, with the *Limbun nang San José*, where replicas of woodworking tools are borne in the town's longest procession.

The exuberant Betis central retablo dates from the 2nd half of the 18th century.

Parish Church of St. William of Aquitaine (San Guillermo de Aquitania)

Brgy. Cabambangan, Bácolor, 2001
Pampanga, Philippines
Feast day: February 10 (San Guillermo);
Third Sunday of November (Virgen de la Naval)
Archdiocese of San Fernando, Pampanga

Organized by the Augustinians in 1576, Bácolor (from *bakulud*, "elevated land") quickly progressed as it lay along important commercial routes. It was the capital of Pampanga from 1755 to 1904.

An adobe stone church begun in the 17th century was constantly renovated in the next two centuries. The baroque façade of the church was remodeled possibly in the 1930's. Elements from its original style, however, may be seen in the transepts, through the unique brickwork series of hollow rectangles and triangles outlining their pediments, and the stout buttress-like volutes flanking the openings. The convento was considered the largest in the province.

From 1991 to 1995 the town began to be mired in lahar flows from the eruption of Mount Pinatubo. The community doggedly kept vigil by the church, which has since been rehabilitated in accordance with the raised floor level.

In the early 1990s lahar from Pinatubo mired the buildings, originally from the 17th century, so that one enters through what was once the central window of the choir loft.

Image of Santo Tomás de Villanueva, in a sumptuously carved niche

Today's ceiling has been removed, giving a "lift" to the space while exposing the massive trusswork. The lahar ground has been tiled and the retablos are newly polychromed and gilded.

The central retablo is 19th century neoclassic. On the uppermost niche is the image of the patron saint, William of Aquitaine (often confused with William the Hermit). Below him is Our Lady of the Rosary of La Naval, whose feast-day is celebrated on the third Sunday of November. (According to tradition, this date gave devotees enough time to celebrate her fiesta in the original shrine in Santo Domingo, Manila, on the second Sunday of October.) The 18th century transept retablos exemplify some tour-de-force carving, even by baroque standards. The columns are wound with vines so masterfully cut that one can curl a finger around the tendrils. The flanges are pierced and not solid like a bas-relief, so that light passing through gives a lace-like effect. The curved niche behind the figure of Saint Augustine in the left retablo is also carved in the rear (does this suggest that it may have been turned around to cover the image during "ordinary" seasons?). The retablo on the right has the same open-work flanges but not the columns. Could the carved pieces be all that remained of a previous altarpiece? And what happened to the original baroque retablo in the sanctuary that would have been contemporary with those in the transept?

One can hardly tell that the church is two-thirds its height—except for the curious sensation that by jumping a little higher one can reach the roof.

The interior has beautifully accommodated the lower roofline.

Parish Church of Our Lady of Mt. Carmel

Barasoain, Malolos City, 3000
Bulacan, Philippines
Feast day: July 16
Diocese of Malolos

Undoubtedly, no other Philippine church has been so reproduced on paper as that of Barasoain, Bulacan. It appeared on a stamp issued in 1935. After 1945, it was depicted on the 10-peso bill, and then on the 200-peso bill (since 2010). A 2,000-peso bill was specially issued in 1998 to commemorate both a presidential swearing into office at Barasoain and the centennial of Philippine independence.

Before Barasoain became so famous, it was a district of Malolos, the capital of Bulacan province. It was established as a town and parish in 1859, and named after a town in Navarra, Spain. Its first chapel was that of the cemetery separated from the mother town by a stream. After a fire, an earthquake, and another fire, construction of the present church of adobe stone was begun in 1885. The project was carried out under the direction of the Augustinian priest Juan Girón, with Miguel Magpayo as foreman. Both their names are inscribed on the pediment (this is a rare incident where a native's contribution to a building is publicly credited). Although the receding arched portal of the façade is characteristic of the Romanesque, the overall style was referred to in the 19th century as *compuesto*. The belltower was rebuilt in 1889.

The combination of elements from various artistic periods led to the composite or *compuesto* style, which aptly describes churches like Barasoain built in the late 19th century.

Pediment with the names of the church's builders

On 15 September 1898, the revolutionary government under General Emilio Aguinaldo convened its first congress in Barasoain church. The first democratic constitution in Southeast Asia was ratified on 23 January 1899 in the church bedecked with palm fronds and Philippine flags.

The Americans never recognized the newly independent Philippine republic especially after the Philippine-American War broke out on 4 February 1899. They pursued Aguinaldo. The fleeing revolutionaries put the churches of Malolos and Barasoain to the torch before these towns fell on 31 March 1899.

Repair and recognition came gradually. In 1989, the wooden altarpiece in the sanctuary was removed, exposing once again the original masonry retablo in a simple neoclassic style. Extensive renovations in time for the 100th anniversary of Philippine independence in 1998 replaced the old roof with tiles (but the trusses disappeared), and laid out the black-and-white checkerboard design on the floor as seen in vintage photographs.

Some churches in the far islands have copied Barasoain's familiar façade. Although imposed by unimaginative planners, hopefully the icon will recall what was—or still has to be—achieved in God's country.

The original neoclassic retablo mayor's historicity was altered by recent faux-baroque accretions.

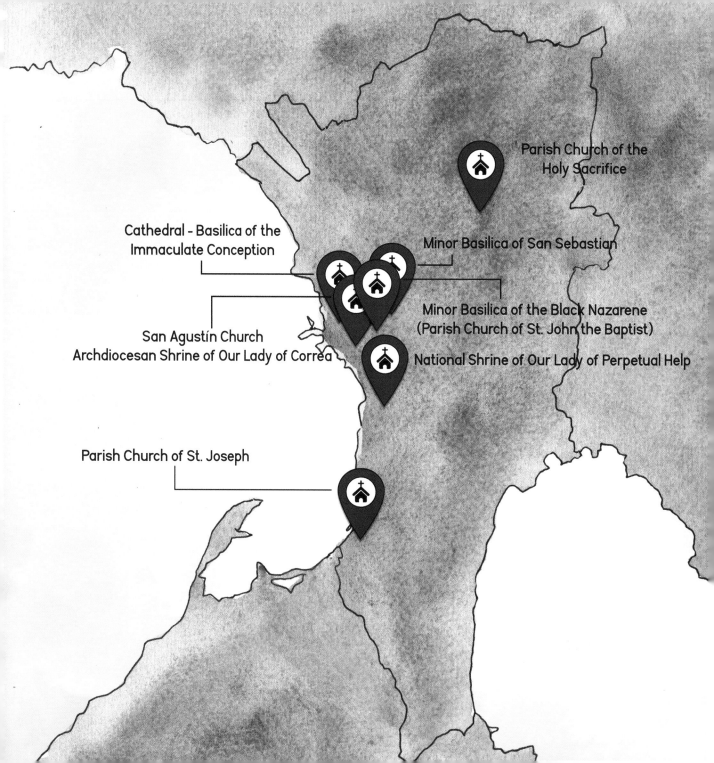

Parish Church of the Holy Sacrifice

Cathedral - Basilica of the Immaculate Conception

Minor Basilica of San Sebastian

San Agustín Church
Archdiocesan Shrine of Our Lady of Correa

Minor Basilica of the Black Nazarene
(Parish Church of St. John the Baptist)

National Shrine of Our Lady of Perpetual Help

Parish Church of St. Joseph

SECTION FOUR: GREATER MANILA AREA

Manila's founding in 1571 by the Spaniards connected the continents in a sustained network of cultures; thus it is acknowledged as the first global city. Its walled enclave, Intramuros, and suburbs housed the mother churches of the religious congregations that evangelized both in the country and in other parts of Asia.

Separated from Mexico as a diocese in 1579, Manila was raised to an archdiocese in 1595, with four suffragans (Nueva Segovia, Nueva Cáceres, Cebu and later Jaro) covering the rest of the country. It has risen from the ashes of 1945, although much of its church heritage was irretrievably lost.

SECTION FOUR: Greater Manila Area

Parish Church of the Holy Sacrifice

J.P. Laurel St., U.P. Diliman Campus, Quezon City, 1104
Metro Manila, Philippines
Feast day: Feast of the Body and Blood of Christ
(Corpus Christi, 10 Sundays after Easter)
Diocese of Cubao

In early 1949, the University of the Philippines moved from its war-torn buildings along Padre Faura Street in Manila to Diliman, Quezon City. When various Christian groups requested the university for a place for their worship services, they were assigned a stable which was the former inter-faith chapel that had been used by the US Army Signal Corps during the war. The rehabilitated shed of split-bamboo walls served as the venue for the services of the Catholics in the morning, Protestants at noon, and Aglipayans in the afternoon. In 1954, Protestants moved to a new church nearby. It was designed by Cesar Concio.

Father John Patrick Delaney was the Jesuit chaplain credited by many to have "Christianized" U.P. Under his guidance, a new church was planned a short distance from the old one. The plan of a round church by Leandro Locsin jived with Delaney's ideas of minimizing the distance between the congregation and the celebrant, antedating Vatican II. (The first round church in the country was actually built in the late 19th century in Piô, Porac, Pampanga.)

The congregation contributed all it could for the construction. They formed a group of the "Holy Thousand" who heard mass everyday until its completion. They performed in the Faculty Follies fund-raiser. They sacrificed their cigarettes, contributed broken bottles for the concrete. They knelt for fair weather during the pouring of the concrete for the thin-shell dome which took 18 hours. On 20 December 1955, after five months of construction, the church was blessed.

The daringly modern Catholic church at the University of the Philippines in Diliman was blessed in 1955—several years ahead of the Second Vatican Council (1962-1965).

Abueva's *Dead and Resurrected Christ* (in a priest's alb)

Locsin, freshly graduated from the University of Santo Tomás, chose the artists to decorate the church with the concurrence of Delaney: Vicente Manansala (assisted by Ang Kiukok), for the Stations of the Cross; Arturo Luz, for the "River of Life" terrazzo flowing from the altar to the sides, and the design of the pews and communion rail; and Napoleon Abueva, for the double crucifix of the Dead Christ and the Risen Christ (and the later marble altar). Jovita Fuentes conducted the church choir, while Felipe P. de Leon conducted the youth choir. José Maceda's avant-garde *Pagsamba* ("Worship") was premiered here in 1968. All these eight in their autumn years were declared National Artists.

The innovative engineers included David Consunji, Alfredo Juinio, Felisberto Reyes, Lamberto Ocampo, and José Segovia.

Not in keeping with the original idea but for security reasons, the perimeter has been fenced. Among the gardens are trees planted in memory of loved ones.

The elevated dome allows natural light and fresh breezes to enhance a worship space that has as little walls as possible.

SECTION FOUR: Greater Manila Area

Cathedral-Basilica of the Immaculate Conception

Cabildo cor. Beaterio St., Intramuros, Manila 1002
Metro Manila, Philippines
Feast day: December 8
Archdiocese of Manila

From the erection of Manila as a diocese in 1579, at least eight cathedrals have arisen on the same site. The first three did not last long. The fourth (1648-1751), burdened with 10 to 12 layers of roof tiles, was replaced by the fifth which was inaugurated in 1760. This had an international character: plans by a visiting Italian priest, Juan de Uguccioni, who also brought with him masons and stones from India; a foreman from Peru; lead and glass from Java; copper grills from Canton. The façade, along baroque Roman lines, fell in the 1852 earthquake.

The sixth cathedral re-opened in 1858, with a neoclassic façade by Nicolás Valdés; but the earthquake of 1863 necessitated so much demolition that a new building was commenced in 1871. (The debris was dumped on the beach, reclaiming land for the avenue that would lead to the Luneta.) The plans by Vicente Serrano Salaverri—drawing on Romanesque, Byzantine and "Oriental" motifs such as pineapples—were carried out by Eduardo López Navarro, Manuel Ramírez y Bazán, and Ramón Hermosa. (Three of the larger-than-life figures of saints on the façade carved by Sotero García are now at the Archdiocesan Museum.)

The seventh cathedral, inaugurated in 1879, survived the 1880 earthquake, proving the efficacy of lessons learned from 1863. Only the belltower, built in 1706 by Dionisio Saplan, collapsed.

The 1879 façade was restored in the 1958 reconstruction of the Manila Cathedral. A modern belltower replaced the one that collapsed in 1863, but the 1706 cupola was replicated.

Symbols of Saint Peter in the choir loft, survivors from 1945

In 1898, the cathedral was used as a military hospital and prison by American troops. During the Liberation of Manila from the Japanese in 1945, the cathedral all but perished.

After much hesitation, the eighth cathedral was rebuilt, and ceremoniously blessed in 1958. Under the direction of Fernando Ocampo, the 1879 façade and about a third of the 1750s plan were retained, from the curved back of the sanctuary (including the two exits to the street) to the transept. The dome was copied from the Duomo of Florence, a nod to the birthplace of Uguccioni.

Several artworks were commissioned from Italy, such as the bronze doors (Rome), marble floors (Carrara), and mosaics (Ravenna). Filipino artist Galo Ocampo designed most of the stained-glass windows, which depict Marian themes and theological concepts—many with a local touch.

A major restoration was undertaken in 2014, in time for the visit of Pope Francis in 2015. The *galeros* or red hats of former cardinals are suspended from the ceiling.

The baldaquin and several art pieces are from the International Institute of Liturgical Art in Rome.

San Agustin Church/ Archdiocesan Shrine of Our Lady of Correa

181 General Luna St., Intramuros, Manila, 1002
Metro Manila, Philippines
Feast day: August 28
Archdiocese of Manila

The Augustinians who had traveled with Legazpi to establish Manila built their first church in 1571. Preliminary studies suggest that the church in its present site was outside the original palisade of the city, and was incorporated when the stone walls were built. The present church of stone was begun in 1586 and concluded in 1604, but occasional fires and earthquakes necessitated its constant renovation. Traces of the early building are the "rusticated" frames of quadrangular blocks around doors and windows. In 1762, British forces sacked the church for 14 days. Some of the lost books were later acquired by the Lilly Library in Indiana, U.S.A. Remains of Legazpi and other founders of Manila were transferred to the chapel left of the sanctuary. The adjoining monastery complex is from the 17th century, with later additions.

The façade has been plastered and de-plastered several times. On the church doors are images of San Agustín and Santa Mónica in late 18th century rococo frames. (Japanese sentries in 1942 sawed off the lower right door so their machine guns could cut down anyone crossing the road.) Two towers were raised in 1854 by Luciano Oliver, architect of Taal Basilica.

The frontage of San Agustín has been remodeled several times since its conclusion in 1604. Of the two towers raised in 1854, the left one had to be torn down after the 1880 earthquake.

Original wall colors behind the pipe organ

A good way to appreciate the church is to view the nave from the choir, passing through the monastery entrance opposite the façade, ascending the granite stairway (and marveling at the brick cupola above), then going all the way to the end at the left. Much of the décor, such as the central retablo, the chandeliers from Paris, and the fool-the-eye painting on the walls (by Italian opera scenery painters), is from the second half of the 19th century. The retablo to the right of the sanctuary enshrines Our Lady of the Correa, the patroness of the Augustinians. Vestiges from earlier centuries are the elaborate pulpit (1627) and 18th century baroque retablos in the crypto-collateral or side chapels, whose walls double as inner buttresses.

The choir loft is distinguished by the carved and inlaid choirstalls and the early 18th century *facistol* or revolving lectern. When the pipe organ was installed in the early 19th century, it concealed the original bright colors, including gilding, on the walls: some of these may be discerned through the peephole behind the organ.

The museum and library safeguard four centuries of culture. A pantheon honors those massacred in 1945.

The interior of San Agustín received a neoclassic theme in the 19th century.

Minor Basilica of San Sebastian

Plaza del Carmen, Quiapo, Manila 1001
Metro Manila, Philippines
Feast day: July 16 (Our Lady of Mt. Carmel)
Archdiocese of Manila

The Augustinian Recollects established the church and convento of San Sebastian in 1621 as a place for convalescence and recollection away from Manila. It was in a community near Quiapo named Calumpang, after a tree whose red fruits yielded oil for lamps. A few months later an image of Our Lady of Mount Carmel was enshrined in the simple church. It had been gifted to the Recollects by the Discalced Carmelite nuns of Mexico City in 1618.

After having had their church destroyed by a fire in 1641 and the earthquakes of 1645, 1863 and 1880, the Recollects approved in 1883 the blueprints for a steel church by Manila's Director of Public Works, Genaro Palacios y Guerra. The engineer, who donated his plans to the Order, had doubtless learned about the new technology through his involvement with the Santolan water system and the port of Manila. After much searching, the Recollects signed a contract for the realization of Palacios' plan in 1886 with the Société Anonyme d'Enterprises de Travaux Publics, which had foundries in Binche, Belgium. From 1888 to 1890, eight ships bearing 1,527 tons of steel parts left Antwerp for Manila. The French engineer Magin Pers (who was simultaneously designing lighthouses) supervised the laying of the complex foundation.

San Sebastian, blessed in 1891, is the first prefabricated structure in the country. Its Plaza del Carmen was regarded as the most beautiful in Manila.

An English engineer, Frederick H. Sawyer—with two Belgian assistants—oversaw the assembly of the edifice (he also constructed the church's iron communion rail). The stained glass was ordered from Linnich, Germany, the chandeliers from Paris, additional lumber from Mindoro, and marble fonts from Romblon. Decoration of the church was by artists from the Academy of Painting and Sculpture. Most of the retablos and furnishings were designed by Lorenzo Guerrero and carved by Eulogio García Velarde. Lorenzo Rocha and his students painted the walls.

The mammoth, earthquake neo-Gothic project was ceremoniously blessed on 15 August 1891.

Although highly popularized, there is no documentary evidence for Gustave Eiffel's involvement with San Sebastian. Credit rests with Genaro Palacios, who offered a pair of *taclobo* giant clams as holy water stoups in the Marian sanctuary of the Montaña in Cáceres, Spain, to coincide with the benediction of his masterpiece in 1891.

Across the church stands the motherhouse of the Augustinian Recollect Sisters. It grew out of the hut given by the friars in 1725 to two feisty sisters, Dionisia and Cecilia Talangpaz. They had left their hometown in Calumpit, Bulacan to be the first native Filipinas admitted into the Recollects' Third Order.

The cupola: steel as stone

The neo-Gothic retablos and fittings were designed and crafted by the most renowned local artists.

MINOR BASILICA OF THE BLACK NAZARENE (PARISH CHURCH OF ST. JOHN THE BAPTIST)

910 Plaza Miranda, Quiapo, Manila 1001
Metro Manila, Philippines
Feast day: June 24; January 9 (Black Nazarene)
Archdiocese of Manila

Quiapo is said to have been named after the eponymous water lettuce that floated on the *esteros* (estuaries) that divided the district into a handful of islands. The estero de Quiapo still runs just about two blocks east of the church. Others have since been filled up, contributing to perennial flooding. Ecclesiastically, Quiapo received its first Franciscan minister in 1586, upon the instigation of the future San Pedro Bautista. In 1598 it was turned over to the Archdiocese for its chancery, and except for a Jesuit interlude in the 1630s, Quiapo has always been administered by the Secular clergy.

A stone church damaged by the 1863 earthquake was rebuilt by 1889. After a fire in 1929, the church was redesigned in the neo-baroque style by Juan Nakpil, who added the second belltower on the left. Much of the ornateness, except for the façades and dome, disappeared in the extension directed by José Ma. Zaragoza in the 1980s.

The neo-baroque frontages and dome of the Quiapo church, as rebuilt in the 1930s, were retained in the 1984 renovation.

Quiapo's Ground Zero is Nuestro Padre Jesús Nazareno (Our Father Jesus the Nazarene), a life-sized image of Jesus Christ genuflecting as he bears a cross on the way to Calvary. Countless devotees draw their faith from his underdog suffering, true grit, and above all his dark color. A documented history of the icon, garbed in maroon and constantly rubbed with balsam oil, has still to be undertaken. The Nazareno is believed to have been brought from Mexico in the 17th century, and housed with the Augustinian Recollects, first in their church in Bagumbayan and then within Intramuros. A confraternity was established to foment devotion to the Nazarene in 1608. The image was entrusted to Quiapo by Archbishop Sancho during his reign from 1767-1787.

Due to the wear and tear of generations of processions (the *traslación* capping the January 9 fiesta reached up to 22 hours in the past four years), two images have been created. The statue at the central altar keeps the head of the original, while the battle-scarred body (with a new head) is the one brought out of the church.

A number of Quiapo's curates are historical figures. Hernando de los Ríos, who guided the carving of the venerated icon of La Naval in the 1590s, was a cleric here in 1603. Bartolomé Saguinsin eulogized the defense of Manila against the British, in classic Latin verse published in 1766. Others were patriots, while five of them became bishops.

The mid-20th century baldaquin by Maximo Vicente, Jr., prevails over the modernistic gym-like space.

Pagpupuri

Matamis na sinta na pinahirapan Jesus na buhay co't aquing cagalingan:
Coro: O arao sa lupa at sang Langitan, maguing Ama ca po namin at tangulang.

Ang tao'y nang iyong mangyaring malalang ay pinuspos mo pa niyaong cagalingan;
at nang maquita mong na sa casalanan pinilit mong tubsin nang dugo mong mahal.
O arao sa lupa at sang Langitan, maguing Ama ca po namin at tangulang.

Ang pagsinta mo po'y di nga maulatan, nanaog sa Langit ang lupa'y linacbay,
hanggang mapaco ca't sa Cruz mamatay, at maguing dagat nang dusa't cahirapan.
O arao sa lupa at sang Langitan, maguing Ama ca po namin at tangulang.

Nagpatirapá sa iyong paa-nan na ang hingi nami'y huag pagcaitan
nang bungang masarap ng Pasión mong mahal, alang alang doon sa lualhating taglay.
O arao sa lupa at sang Langitan, maguing Ama ca po namin at tangulang.

O Jesus nang aquing calolouang tangan, o pangalang Jesús, catamistamisan,
mapagbigay ca nga sa tauo nang buhay at sa panininta'y uala cang cabagay.
O arao sa lupa at sang Langitan, maguing Ama ca po namin at tangulang.

Masintahin Dios cami ay tunghayan nang mga matá mong may dating hinayang,
at caming Anac mo ay ipagsangalang yamang Ama cangang lubos caauá an.
O arao sa lupa at sang Langitan, maguing Ama ca po namin at tangulang.

Excerpt from *Novena sa Caibigibig na Poon Nating Jesús Nazareno Pintacasing Sinasamba sa Simbahan nang Quiapo Sacop nang Maynila,* Tagalog translation by Don Jose Maria Guevara, parish priest of Quiapo; first published in 1870, of the Spanish original by Doctor Don Luis Hocson, published in 1810.
Archivo de la Universidad de Santo Tomás, Manila

Praises

My sweet tormented love, Jesus, my life and well-being:
Refrain: Oh sun over heaven and earth, be our Father and Protector.

When you created humankind out of nothing, you filled him with goodness;
but seeing him fall into sin you made haste to redeem him with your precious blood.
Refrain: Oh sun over heaven and earth, be our Father and Protector.

Your love is so immense that you came down from heaven, even to die on the Cross, a sea of pain and suffering.
Refrain: Oh sun over heaven and earth, be our Father and Protector.

We fell on our knees asking not to be denied the sweet fruit of your glorious Passion.
Refrain: Oh sun over heaven and earth, be our Father and Protector.

Oh Jesus of my soul, Oh sweetest name of Jesus, giving life to man, in loving you have no equal.
Refrain: Oh sun over heaven and earth, be our Father and Protector.

Loving God, turn to us with compassionate eyes, and protect us your children since you Our Father are truly merciful.
Refrain: Oh sun over heaven and earth, be our Father and Protector.

Nuestro Padre Jesús Nazareno, Christ on his way to crucifixion

NATIONAL SHRINE OF OUR LADY OF PERPETUAL HELP

Redemptorist Road, Baclaran, 1702 Parañaque City
Metro Manila, Philippines
Feast day: June 27
Diocese of Parañaque

Members of the Congregation of the Most Holy Redeemer (C.Ss.R., or Redemptorists) from Australia commenced the construction of their house and a wooden church in Baclaran, a fishing village of Parañaque, in 1931. They would have procured their seafood from the nearby *baclad* or traps planted on the shores of Manila Bay (which today is two kilometers away). The rural setting of the property, donated by a certain "Anastasia," was ideal for their apostolate of building Christian communities.

The idyll changed after the introduction of the first perpetual novena to Our Mother of Perpetual Help on Wednesday, 23 June 1948. It was led by Father Leo James English. (He compiled an English-Tagalog dictionary years later.) From an initial attendance of 70 persons, the novena now attracts up to 150,000 devotees on Wednesdays.

The devotion may have been inadvertently promoted when the media blew up a story that roses had been found by an altar boy, relating it to the alleged scattering of rose petals in the Carmel Monastery in Lipa in late 1948. The common people readily related to the collective petitions in the novena, which has been updated to include concerns like social and environmental justice.

The modern church of Baclaran was built over the old wooden one and was blessed in 1958 after six years of construction. Devotees light candles in the pavilion to the right.

The patronal icon, first brought by the Redemptorists to the Philippines in 1906, is a copy of a painting in the Byzantine style, carbon-dated to between 1323 and 1480. It is said to have been brought from Crete to Rome, where it has been venerated in the Redemptorists' church since 1866. It represents Mary comforting the Child Jesus, who seems to have rushed into her arms upon being presented the symbols of his Passion and Cross by Saints Michael (left) and Gabriel (right).

The present airy church (built 1953-1958) was designed by architect Cesar Concio and his associate Jesse Bontoc. People donated ten centavos a week for its construction. Although described as "Modern Romanesque," venturing further than its cousins Santo Domingo (1954) and Manila Cathedral (1954-1958), its façade recalls the neo-Baltic Gothic Grundtvig's church (1927-1940) in Copenhagen, Denmark. The Carillon was inaugurated in 2015.

Saint John Paul II, when still archbishop of Kraków, stopped by Baclaran in 1973 and was ennobled by the full church at a late hour. In 1981, as pope, he returned to Baclaran where he addressed the women religious of the country (with Mother Teresa in attendance). He entrusted his apostolic tour of the Far East to Our Lady's care.

Criss-crossing bronze wheat stalks support the tabernacle.

NOVENA PRAYER

Dear Mother of Perpetual Help, from the cross Jesus gave you to us for our Mother.
You are the kindest, the most loving of all mothers.
Look tenderly on us your children as we now ask you to help us in all our needs especially this one
(Pause to recall your petitions).

While you were on earth, dear Mother, you willingly shared in the sufferings of your Son.
Strengthened by your faith and confidence in the fatherly love of God,
you accepted the mysterious designs of His Will.
We, too, have our crosses and trials. Sometimes they almost crush us to the ground.

Dearest Mother, share with us your abundant faith and confidence in God.
Make us aware that God never ceases to love us;
that He answers all our prayers in the way that is best for us.
Strengthen our hearts to carry the cross in the footsteps of your Divine Son.
Help us to realize that he who shares the cross of Christ will certainly share His resurrection.

Dearest Mother, as we worry about our own problems let us not forget the needs of others.
You always love others so much; help us to do the same.
While praying for our own intentions and for the intentions of all here present at this Novena
we earnestly ask you, our Mother to help us comfort the sick and the dying,
give hope to the poor and unemployed, heal the broken-hearted, walk in solidarity with the oppressed,
teach justice to their oppressors, and bring back to God all those who have offended Him.

Dearest Mother, help us to avoid sin which separates us from our heavenly Father
and from one another. Full of trust in you we place ourselves under the mantle of your
maternal protection and confidently hope for your compassionate intercession. Amen.

Excerpted from the *2016 Revised English Novena,* National Shrine of Our Mother of Perpetual Help, Baclaran,
Parañaque City

The likeness of Our Mother of Perpetual Help, a copy of the 14th -15th century Cretan icon now venerated in Rome

Parish Church of St. Joseph

**Padre Diego Cera Avenue, Brgy. Daniel Fajardo,
Las Piñas City, 1742
Metro Manila, Philippines
Feast day: First Sunday of May
Diocese of Parañaque**

Las Piñas was separated ecclesiastically from Parañaque in 1775. Augustinian Recollect Diego Cera was its first parish priest. He built the present church of adobe from 1797 to 1819. Lime for the masonry was obtained from *talabá*, the local oysters.

Another distinguished curate of Las Piñas was Ezequiel Moreno (1876-1879), who was canonized in 1992. He is remembered for having spent many times of prayer in the choir loft, and for having miraculously stopped a fire from spreading in 1879.

The church was buttressed after the earthquakes of 1880. From 1913 until very recently, the parish was ministered to by the Belgian priests of the Congregation of the Immaculate Heart of Mary (C.I.C.M). During the rehabilitation of the church and convento (1962-1977), the protective *palitada* layer was removed. This also resulted in the discovery of Diego Cera's cipher on the arch over the choir loft, as well as another which may read, "Don Bernardo Mateo," possibly a foreman or mayor of the time.

Even before the foundations were dug for the church of Las Piñas in 1797, Father Diego Cera had formed a small orchestra of violins and basses. Mass was first said in 1811 in the baptistry, until the church was completed in 1819.

In 1816 bamboo selected for the town's now famous pipe organ were buried in the sand for a year to render them unappetizing to insects. Completed in 1824, it bore the Spanish royal crown with its diamonds and ovals on its case. Spanish too was the manner in which the organ was installed to one side of the choir loft (so the organist could time his music with the service); as was the *trompetería*, the tin reed pipes projecting horizontally. 902 of the 1,031 pipes are of bamboo. There are 22 stops or registers manipulated from either side of the keyboard. There is one stop for bird sounds, and another for the drum (produced by the two largest pieces of bamboo).

It is assumed that Cera learned his craft as he grew up in Aragón. A year after his arrival in Manila in 1792, he is credited with having constructed a forte-piano fit for the queen of Spain; he was instrumental in the building or improvement of the organs in his order's mother church San Nicolás in 1794 (with one stop of bamboo); the Manila cathedral (1804); San Agustín (1814); Argao, Cebu (1816?); and Báclayon, Bohol (1824). His typical tripartite case construction was brought by his disciples to several Augustinian Recollect-administered parishes in Bohol, between 1830 and 1850.

The restoration of the bamboo organ (1973-1975) in Bonn, Germany, gave rise to the internationally acclaimed Bamboo Organ Festival, held every February. The instrument is maintained by the Diego Cera Organ Builders, Inc.

The Bamboo Organ, built from 1816 to 1824

In the 1816, the Augustinian Recollects donated the retablo mayor of stone.

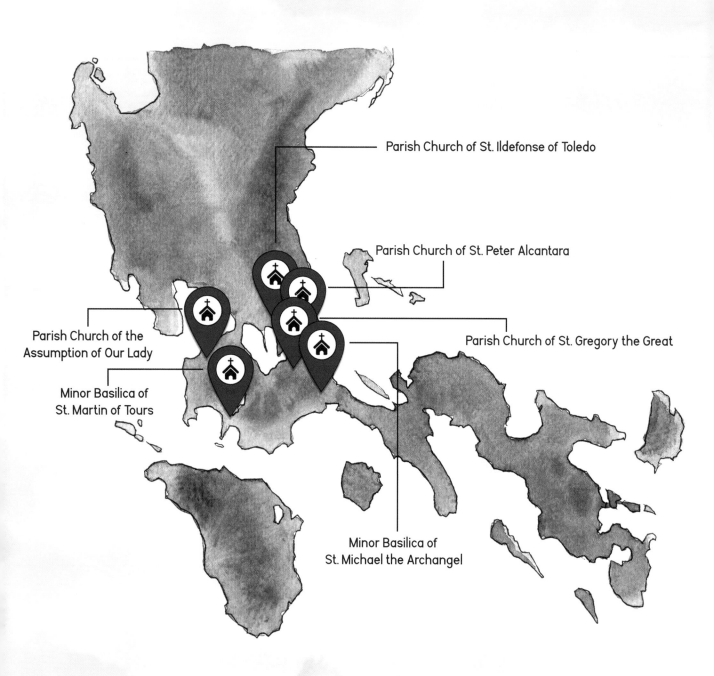

Parish Church of St. Ildefonse of Toledo

Parish Church of St. Peter Alcantara

Parish Church of the
Assumption of Our Lady

Parish Church of St. Gregory the Great

Minor Basilica of
St. Martin of Tours

Minor Basilica of
St. Michael the Archangel

SECTION FIVE: SOUTHWESTERN LUZON

The peoples south and east of Manila were Tagalogs like their counterparts north of the city. The Augustinians pioneered missions in the area in 1572 in Taal and San Mateo. The Franciscans commenced their apostolate in 1578 around Laguna de Bay with Morong, Pila, and Lumbang, and beyond with Tayabas and Lucban. Their missions in Antipolo, Cavite and western Batangas were turned over to the Jesuits in the 1590s.

When the Jesuits left in 1768, their parishes were turned over to the Seculars, and then to the Augustinian Recollects. Most of the area today is spiritually administered by the Seculars.

Parish Church of St. Ildefonse of Toledo

M.H. Del Pilar, Brgy. Plaza Aldea, Tanay, 1980
Rizal, Philippines
Feast day: January 23
Diocese of Antipolo

Tanay was founded as a town separate from Pililla in 1606. From the slopes of Mount Tanay it transferred in 1620 to a site some 3 kilometers further north, but in 1640 it descended to its present location by the lake and an eponymous river. Church buildings of stone were concluded in 1680, financed largely from votive offerings to a miraculous image of the Virgin. A larger church and convento replaced these in 1783.

The church plaza is shaded by centennial acacias; the central one, toppled by a typhoon, was carved into a massive monument. Both church and convento are of adobe blocks, durable enough to have withstood the centuries without *palitada*. Both the main and left side façades are delicately carved. The sinuous volutes flanking the upper niches on both façades are the last vestiges of the baroque, transcended by the rococo in the interior. The canopies behind Saints Francis and Dominic flanking the main entrance are supposed to be the standard clamshells but also recall lotus petals. Pineapples punctuate both ends of the pediment.

The church and convento of Tanay were built in the 1780s of a superior type of adobe that did not require *palitada*, which then allowed for fine carving. The stone image of the patron, San Ildefonso de Toledo, keeps watch from the highest niche of the pediment.

Image of San Pedro Bautista, one of the Franciscan martyrs of Japan

All six retablos at the apse, transept, and baptistry of the church, as well as the pulpit, ostentate irregular shapes that resemble bubbles enclosed by flames—motifs diagnostic of the rococo.

The central image of San Ildefonso on the main retablo (1785-1786) is backlit by a window. In front of the left retablo is a wooden tabernacle that may date to the previous church. Left of this retablo is another dedicated to Our Lady of Anguish, based on a prototype in Granada Cathedral, Spain. The retablo to the right of the sanctuary carries images of two Franciscans martyred in Nagasaki, Japan: San Pedro Bautista, crucified in 1597, and Beato Bartolomé Laurel, burned alive in 1627.

Another treasure of the church is the set of fourteen bas-relief stations of the cross that line both sides of the nave. The first twelve, as well as the five bas-reliefs on the top levels of the central and side retablos, are by the same archaic hand. The unknown master has incorporated many interesting details: writing instruments, bladed weapons, even (sun?) glasses. Curiously, the mustached soldiers in the first station appear clean shaven for the rest of the series.

The convento, like those of the Franciscans in this area, completely encloses a courtyard. Both levels are of stone, without a *volada* or continuous balcony typical of similar colonial edifices

The central retablo and five others in the church, together with the pulpit, benches, and the stone fonts (now behind the belltower) form the largest ensemble of rococo ecclesiastical furnishings in the country.

Parish Church of the Assumption of Our Lady

Población 1A, Maragondon, 4112
Cavite, Philippines
Feast day: August 15
Diocese of Imus

The church complex in Maragondon is one of the most complete that was built and decorated by the Jesuits in the Philippines, although there were also significant contributions by their successors, the diocesan clergy (1768-1885), the Augustinian Recollects (1885-1898), and again the diocesan clergy (1898-present). The town had its Christian beginnings under the Franciscans in the early 1600s. About 1611 or 1614, it separated from Silang as an independent ministry under the Society of Jesus.

The majority of the present church with its stout pilaster-buttresses, the belltower, and the inner walls of the convento, are of rubblework. It may be hazarded that these were begun in 1687, and only concluded in 1714. At some point in the 18th or 19th century, cut stone was used for the amplification of the buttresses, the raising of the height of the façade, and major renovations in the convento.

Recent work on the façade has revealed the rubblework dating from about 1687 to 1714, and the cut stonework of the pediment added in about 1840. The belltower, unique for the multiple demarcations as it tapers to the top, commands a good view of the river from which the stone was quarried.

Retablo detail: an angel blowing on a carabao horn *tambuli*

From the Jesuit era are the three ornate baroque retablos and pulpit. The two side retablos incorporate parts that may have been sourced from earlier altarpieces. The one on the left, more sober, may have enshrined the Santo Niño brought by islanders from Ternate, Indonesia, in 1663 until the independence of their own parish in 1863. The one on the right has four twisted columns that are smaller copies of those in Silang, Cavite; the two upper columns don't even properly match. The *portaciriales* (pedestals for processional candleholders) in the form of kneeling angels in kimonos knotted in front are cousins of those in Guiuan, Samar. A crucifix dated 1712 is found near the main entrance. The magnificently carved doors resemble those in Indang (Cavite) and Báclayon (Bohol).

The trusses that hold the nave in place are inscribed with praises to the Madonna. The one over the choir loft records when it was installed—April 17, 1842—and the name of the parish priest, Don Anastacio de los Reyes, who ministered from 1837 to 1855. The secular priests spiritually administered Maragondon for 117 years, the longest under the Manila archdiocese in Spanish Cavite.

Upon their assumption of the parish in 1885, the Augustinian Recollects fitted the windows with colored glass panes and topped them with medallions depicting the symbols of their patron in the Philippines, San Nicolás de Tolentino. These include a belt, stars, and a partridge on a plate. A horseshoe-shaped communion rail with parquetry footing, like that in San Sebastian (Manila), was also installed.

The baroque retablo dates from the early 18th or late 17th century. In the middle tier, the patronal image of Our Lady of the Assumption is flanked on the left by San Ignacio de Loyola and on the right by San Luis Gonzaga.

PARISH CHURCH OF ST. PETER ALCANTARA

Población, Pakil, 4017
Laguna, Philippines
Feast day: October 19; September 15 (Turumba)
Diocese of San Pablo

The town of Pakil was separated ecclesiastically from Paete in 1676. The present church and convento were built between 1732 and 1767, under the direction of the Franciscans; the mass of the tower dates from 1777. The walls of alternating layers of brick and orange-colored stone blocks are also seen in contemporary southern Tagalog edifices. Extensive repairs were made in 1852 (after a town-wide fire that miraculously left 300 prints of Our Lady of Sorrows barely singed) and in the 1980s.

A small oil painting of Our Lady of Sorrows was fished out of the banks of the Matamig River in 1788, and is now venerated in a chapel in the convento. Seven novenas or *lupî* held for every month of her sorrows lead to the fiesta on the Sunday nearest September 15. A carved representation of this painting is taken from the central retablo, ensconced in an elaborate *andas* (float), and processed throughout the main streets to a march composed by a native son, Marcelo Adonay (whose monument, instead of Rizal in other places, faces the church). Devotees gracefully sway and "fall down" (*tumbá*) to console Our Lady, hence her unique name: Nuestra Señora de los Dolores de Turumba.

The building of the church was concluded in 1767, while the first two floors of the tower were added a decade later. The upper façade, which echoes the decorative scheme of the Franciscan church of Santa Ana, Manila, begun in 1720, contains the image of the patron saint, San Pedro de Alcantara.

The three principal retablos are early to middle 18th century baroque. In the center of the uppermost tier of the main retablo is the patron saint, San Pedro Alcantara, a reformer of the Franciscan order. Below him is the niche reserved for the carved image of Our Lady of Sorrows. The two side retablos appear to be elevated on platforms faced with carved panels; they may have been adapted from an earlier, smaller church. In the uppermost niche of the right retablo is an unidentified Franciscan martyr, rising from the flames.

On the walls of the transept hang two bas-reliefs. One illustrates the conversion of a peasant when a hungry mule knelt in front of the Eucharist held out by San Antonio de Padua, despite the grain provided. The other depicts San Francisco receiving the stigmata of Christ on the eve of the feast of the Exaltation of the Cross (September 14).

Beyond the pulpit and *The Final Judgment*, a mid-19th century painting attributed to José Dans from nearby Paete, is a rococo altarpiece depicting Calvary. The Crucified Christ is rubbed with balsam and adorned with silver before being brought out for the Good Friday procession. By the principal entrance is a local interpretation of a Chinese lion holding up a holy water font.

A Calvary scene framed in rococo, possibly erected after the fire of 1794

The central retablo, from the first half of the 18th century, is typically baroque with its profuse, swirling carved decorations and numerous niches for saints' images.

Parish Church of St. Gregory the Great

F. Blumentritt St., Brgy. Sta. Catalina, Majayjay, 4005
Laguna, Philippines
Feast day: March 12
Diocese of San Pablo

Majayjay on the slopes of Mount Banahaw was an important stop along the alternate route linking Manila to the Pacific and the Bicol peninsula; the more manageable coasts were prone to attacks during the "pirate months." The present church is the sixth of the town, from the first in 1571. Under the direction of the Franciscans, a church of stone built after 1660 was so decrepit by 1707 that it was decided to enclose the walls in brick between 1711 and 1734. The lairs of people who fled from the onerous project were eventually formalized into the towns of Magdalena (1821) and Luisiana (1848). Massive additions to the church, this time using adobe blocks, were the apse, transept, buttresses, portico over the right side entrance, belltower, and convento.

The façade is severely monumental. This contrasts with the right side portal, whose jambs sprout curious knobs over Red Cross-like forms resting on their sides. The octagonal tray design below the niches is repeated on the right side of the interior of the nave, which in turn is much more decorated than the opposite one.

The massiveness of Majayjay's church is due to the sandwiching of the decrepit building with walls that reached a thickness of three meters in 1730. It is said that leaves of the *puso-puso* plant were crushed and mixed with the mortar for added stability.

Portico over the early 18th century right side entrance

Both sides of the nave are provided with benches of masonry; balustered galleries on the upper level give an idea of how much the church was filled up, especially during feast days. A curious balcony perched on an inverted three-lobed pyramid may have supported a pipe organ, except that it coincides with the door to the second level of the convento.

The central retablo is 19th century neoclassic. The two side retablos have a red granolithic finish, and stylistically could be from the early 20th century. Could the earlier 18th century retablos have rotted in the course of several typhoons? Possible remnants of these are the statues and bas-reliefs in the niches along the walls. The bas-reliefs in particular are from the 18th century or even earlier. The presence of two calvary scenes may suggest that one belonged to another church.

The floors of the sanctuary and the baptistry are paved with *azulejo* tiles of various designs. Just outside the latter chamber is the previous baptismal font, dated 1790, relocated after renovations in the 19th century.

Behind the church, a road leads to the Chapel of Nuestra Señora de la Portería. This was the former tribunal, rehabilitated in 1760 to enshrine the eponymous icon from Madrid. Here, Ilayang Majayjay, was the site of the town from 1602 to 1606.

The neoclassic central retablo must have replaced an earlier one, whose original images are possibly those in the niches along the nave.

Minor Basilica of St. Martin of Tours

Marcela M. Agoncillo St., Población, 4208 Taal, Batangas, Philippines
Feast day: November 11
Archdiocese of Lipa

The first Christian mission in Batangas province was founded by the Augustinians in Taal ("authentic" in Tagalog) in 1572, just a year after Manila's establishment. The community moved in 1575 to what is now San Nicolás, on the shore of Taal Lake where it joins the Pansipit (for the *sipit* or tongs) River. At that time the lake was more like a marine bay, but the volcano in the lake's eruptions in the 1750s spewed out so much matter that the connection with the sea shrunk into a river. The Taaleños moved down the river towards the sea; they settled on a plain above Caysasay, whose sanctuary to the Virgin had been saluted by passing galleons since the 1600s.

A cut coralstone church built in the second half of the 18th century was pulled down by about 1853. A new one of adobe was commenced in 1857 for the burgeoning population, with plans by Esteban Nepomuceno Transfiguración of Manila. It was redesigned by the Spanish architect Luciano Oliver and inaugurated in 1865. Work continued until the 1880s under Rafael Janin, another Spanish architect from Manila. Only one of the two towers was completed in 1883; it collapsed in 1942 and was rebuilt a few decades ago.

The neoclassic Taal Basilica is so monumental it is arguably the largest in the country. The Ionic and Corinthian capitals over the double columns are of solid *molave*.

Folksy image of Saint Martin on horseback, on a 19th century bell

Just beyond the rounded apse of the basilica and within the school grounds is the abandoned cemetery. There are 19th century chapels in nearby Balisong (where the eponymous fan knives are sold), and Bagumbayan (new town).

A visit to Taal is not complete without descending the 1840s stairway of granite *piedra China* slabs to visit ancient Caysasay. The church was begun around 1639 to enshrine a diminutive image of the Virgin said to have been fished out from the Pansipit River in 1603. The convento is L-shaped, with the open side towards the plaza, "embracing" pilgrims much like Bernini's colonnade in Rome. Both structures are of cut coralstone, like that used in the Taal convento. A short hike into the hillside leads to the Well of Santa Lucía. Below a gorgeous early 18th century stone arch, devotees fetch healing water for their various ailments.

Ruins of the original church site of Taal still stand in the present town of San Nicolás, just a hundred meters from the lakeshore and less than an hour's drive from today's Taal. The edifice of rows of round brain coral blocks is most possibly the one built by 1630.

The neoclassic main retablo was recently garnished with faux-baroque trimmings.

Minor Basilica of St. Michael the Archangel

Lopez Jaena St., Ilasan, Tayabas, 4301
Quezon, Philippines
Feast day: September 9
Diocese of Lucena

Like Majayjay on the other side of Mount Banahaw, Tayabas was a major crossroads between the eastern and western parts of southern Luzon. Its inhabitants cultivated rice on terraces akin to those in the Cordillera, and spoke Tayabasin, a distinct version of Tagalog. Both church and convento of San Miguel Arcángel of Tayabas have probably been on the bank overlooking the Alitao River for over 400 years.

Initial Christianization by the Franciscans began in 1578, and a stone church was built shortly after 1600. As a defense against pirates the convento, said to date from 1649, was fortified with *troneras* (gun emplacements), which were still visible in the 1860s. The Franciscan printing press was briefly housed here in 1703. Both buildings were constantly enlarged throughout the 18th century, especially after the 1743 earthquake. A new façade with a triangular pediment was constructed in 1761. Between 1850 to 1860, it was reshaped from triangular to semicircular.

From the upper reaches of the façade, the three archangels guard the town. Emerging from the frame of the central window, like the formless body of Casper the friendly ghost, is San Diego de Alcala clutching his penitential cross. (His image in a side altar enjoyed great devotion in the past.) Flanking the main entrance is a pair of Chinese lions as interpreted by indigenous hands: rather lithe, and grinning.

The church, which stands on the same site since at least the 1640s, was enlarged in the middle of the 18th century. The raised façade with a rounded pediment was blessed in 1860.

In the 1850s, the nave was expanded with an apse and transept with rounded ends. Subsequently, the walls were painted and a sacristy was added (1873). During the war, the church was unharmed, but the convento, converted by the Japanese into a garrison, was bombed.

Most of the retablos are 19th century neoclassic. The retablo in the sacristy and the well-polished silver frontal in the sanctuary are late 18th century rococo. The walls were painted in 1925, and later restored. The pipe organ in the choir loft was installed in 1865.

Four *ermitas* (chapels) are distributed throughout the town: San Diego de Alcala (1683, beside the Alitao Bridge southwest of the church); de las Angustias (1728, to the northeast); San Roque (1755, in the cemetery on the road to Lucena), and one for the *cementerio católico* (1887, on the road to Sariaya). A number of bridges built by the Franciscans still survive.

In 1901, after 300 years, the Americans moved the provincial capital from Tayabas to Lucena, a former barrio of the old town.

San Diego de Alcala, like a friendly ghost, on the façade

Constructed at about the same time that the cupola was built (1858-1860), the central retablo is more "animated" than most of its neoclassic contemporaries.

Parish Church of
the Purification of Our Lady
(Nuestra Señora de Candelaria)

Cathedral of
St. John the Evangelist

Parish Church of Our Lady of the Gate
(Nuestra Señora de la Portería)

Parish Church of St. Joseph

SECTION SIX: BICOL

The Christianization of most of the Bicol region was realized by the Franciscans, with their first mission at Naga in 1578. They were intermittently assisted by the Augustinian Recollects and the Seculars, who in the 19th century administered much of the southern and eastern parts.

Many churches were built along the undulating Bicol River (from *biko*, twisted, or *bikul*, a local bamboo). Missions were also established where the *cimarrones* or mountain people were resettled, Peñafrancia being the most famous. The history of church building has been greatly influenced by the active volcanoes in the area such as Mayon and Bulusan.

Parish Church of the Purification of Our Lady (Nuestra Señora de Candelaria)

Paracale, 4605
Camarines Norte, Philippines
Feast day: February 2
Diocese of Daet

Paracale has been synonymous with gold since a 1576 report that informed Philip II of the mines in this town. They say it takes its name from *paracali*, a ditch digger. Although the resulting industry did not live up to its promises until the boomtown of American traders in the 1920s, Catholic missionaries saw a different set of opportunities.

Tentative efforts in 1581 were formalized in 1611, when the Franciscans assigned resident ministers to the first three missions in what is now the province of Camarines Norte: Paracale and its nearest pueblos, Indan (now Vinzons) and Daet. Separated from Paracale were the coastal towns of Capalongan in 1634, then Mambulao (now José María Panganiban) in 1666. Their gold deposits attracted not only prospectors but pirates, who in not a few cases were Tagalog-speaking privateers. Mambulao is derived from *mambulawan*, bountiful with gold.

The present stone church was built by a secular priest who ministered here at least between the years 1839 and 1864. He even placed his name on the façade: Don José Clemente Rosales. The edifice is one of the few in Bicol with two belfries, along with Santo Domingo and Santa Rosa both in Albay.

The triangular icon of the Trinity on the church of Paracale, built in the mid-19th century, is erroneously interpreted by some as a Masonic symbol placed by revolutionaries. This would have necessitated the improbable replacement of the original stones with newly chiseled ones.

Gaunt stone image of San Pablo on the façade

The diocesan clergy were in spiritual charge of Paracale from 1696 to 1880. A native son, Gregorio Cabalquinto, was ordained in 1706 as the earliest-known Bicol priest. Another Paracale-born priest, Patricio Zaño, said his first mass here in 1880. The neo-Gothic side retablos (the central altarpiece is recent) were crafted in that year by his father Don Vicente Zaño.

As befitting the patroness of a town historically famous for its gold, Inay Candi (as Our Lady is fondly called here) is arrayed for her feast day in the eternal metal: from her crown, to the open-work bodice and sleeves (with separate cuffs), to the trimmings on the silver skirt overlay. Her right hand holds a mayor's staff and lighted taper (both of silver), while her left cradles the Holy Infant (not always present on ordinary days). Both images, from the 18th century or earlier, have heads and hands of ivory. Kept in the church is a miniature sword of gold and silver, engraved with the date 29 August 1809. On this day, according to witnesses, a lady brandishing a sword saved the town from a fleet of pirates on 37 canoes. (Two cannon in the plaza recall those dangerous times.)

The central retablo is a modern adaptation of the 1880 neo-Gothic side retablos.

CATHEDRAL OF
ST. JOHN THE EVANGELIST

Elias Angeles St., Naga City, 4400
Camarines Sur, Philippines
Feast day: December 27
Archdiocese of Caceres

Pre-hispanic Naga was located in the area around the present railway station, on the right bank of the eponymous river a short distance from its strategic crossing with the Bicol River; *naga* was a wood from which finely worked cups were made. In 1575 the Spaniards established a settlement across Naga, and named it Cáceres after the reigning governor's birthplace. The pueblo became the seat of the Diocese of Nueva Cáceres in 1595, with jurisdiction over the entire Bicol region. Wedged between the episcopal center and the river grew the Parian, the Chinese district. Old Cáceres and the Parian are now the site of the city's commercial center. On land adjoining Cáceres to the north, the Franciscans founded a church in 1578. A rebuilt brick campanile now stands on the site.

Bishop Bernardo de la Concepción Perdigón (1816-1829) relocated the cathedral to a rice land further up the river, just north of the Franciscans. Within this expanse— reflecting the city's growing prosperity from abaca—he delineated spaces for the cathedral, bishop's palace, and seminary.

Although most of the cathedral was up by 1825, the massive stone edifice was blessed only in 1843. With its Doric capitals and friezes—characteristic of the neoclassic style—the cathedral has little of the "Spanish Romanesque" as it is popularly described. Presently, the exterior sports an unusual dark color.

The cathedral was blessed on 27 April 1843, politically coinciding with the birthday of María Cristina de Borbón, the queen regent of Spain. She was the widow of Fernando VII (1813-1833), whose name appears in the seal on the façade.

Spanish royal seal with the name of Fernando VII

The twin belfries closely recall the 1850s belltower at Daraga, Albay. (One bell, dated 1771 and commissioned by Bishop Antonio de Luna, ended up in Carolina, on the foothills of Isarog.)

To the left of the cathedral is the Holy Rosary Minor Seminary, commissioned by Bishop Francisco Gainza (1862-1879). It was built in 1865 and administered by the Vincentian fathers. Diagonally behind the cathedral is the Universidad de Santa Isabel, which began as a school for girls opened by Bishop Gainza in 1868 and administered by the Daughters of Charity. In 1875 it incorporated the first normal school for ladies not only in the Philippines but in southeast Asia.

The cathedral is the venue for the September devotions for the Divino Rostro (an icon introduced during the cholera epidemic in 1882) and Our Lady of Peñafrancia, whose 1710 image is returned in a fluvial procession to her shrine.

During the term of Archbishop Leonardo Legaspi (1983-2012), the cathedral was exuberantly redecorated in 1988.

Parish Church of Our Lady of the Gate (Nuestra Señora de la Portería)

Sta. Maria St., Daraga, 4501
Albay, Philippines
Feast day: September 8
Diocese of Legazpi

When Daraga was approved as a relocation site for Cagsaua in 1772, a church of stone was begun under the direction of Father Juan Duárez, a Franciscan. A slab dated 1773 was installed in the back of the present edifice, but an adjacent carved frame to commemorate the conclusion was to remain blank. Initially, the petitioners of Cagsaua (whose parish was founded in 1605) cited flooding and landslides from nearby Mayon as their reason for transferring. However, the move was countered by the provincial governor, who even induced others to settle in Budiao in 1786. Only after the fateful eruption of Mayon in 1814 (1,200 fatalities) was the transfer to Daraga realized, and the church on the hill overlooking the devastation was finally completed.

The church, tower, and convento are built of andesitic-basalt rocks spewed by the volcano all over the land. Cut stone was only used for the vertical edges of the buttresses. The façade and the lowest level of the belltower are full of florid carvings, except for the apex of the pediment and the rest of the tower (which may have been the sections left unfinished before 1800).

Although the year 1773 inscribed behind the church marks the commencement of its construction, the edifice was only occupied after the devastating eruption of Mayon in 1814. The fourth level of the belltower was added in 1851.

St. Catherine of Alexandria, secondary patron saint of Cagsaua, on the right side of the entrance

There is no other ensemble like Daraga in Bicol. The artists had a free hand interpreting the motifs, in light relief or simple incisions. The baroque columns recall twisted pastries. Flanges with volutes flank openings but also surmount others. The stones have been recently plastered with lime-wash in a sensitive restoration, following early 1900s photographs. Only the baptistry preserves some polychrome on the cornices and bands radiating from the center of the dome.

The façade is so replete with images of saints and religious symbols (was this another way to attract settlers from the lowland?) that it arguably has no rival in the Philippines. There are the principal saints of Franciscan devotions, the Four Evangelists, the Three Theological Virtues and, unusually, two Madonnas. The cornice of the first level of the tower features the Twelve Apostles. Similar carvings are found on the right side entrance and, inside, the columns of the sanctuary, the left side entrance (remnants), and the baptistry. A Crucified Christ, also of stone and which used to stand in the atrium, is now in a church in Makati.

The ruins of the churches in Cagsaua, rebuilt after 1724, and in short-lived Budiao, begun in 1798, are now archaeological sites.

The twisted columns of the exterior inspired the modern central altarpiece.

Parish Church of St. Joseph

**Pan-Philippine Highway, Barcelona, 4712
Sorsogon, Philippines
Feast day: May 19
Diocese of Sorsogon**

Barcelona in Sorsogon was formed from Danlog and parts of the adjoining towns of Gubat and Bulusan. It was established as a town in 1866, and as a parish in 1868. A stone plaque over the main entrance states that the church was begun in 1874.

The parish priest at this time, who ministered to Barcelona until 1898 was Padre Don Victoriano Domingo, a diocesan priest. His former assignment in Goa, Camarines Sur (1855-1862) doubtlessly inspired his design for the façade. Goa was one of the towns along Lagonoy Gulf, where a number of churches were built along the same lines as Barcelona's: an undulating façade topped by a balustraded belfry-pediment. The style was adopted by churches built by the diocesan clergy (San José, Lagonoy, and Caramoan, also Bato in Catanduanes), as well as by the Franciscans (Sagñay).

The most architecturally developed Spanish-era church in Sorsogon is in Barcelona. Like the churches of Gubat and Juban, most of the walls are built of rubblework covered with *palitada*. Cut stone blocks encase the buttresses and frame the windows. What makes the church stand out is its remarkable façade. One can see from behind that it was built of rubblework, like the rest of the edifice, but later faced with cut stone. Its mass is composed of three vertical planes: the two walls that flank the main entrance are slightly concave, following the neoclassic style popular during the mid-19th century. Above the pediment rises the belfry, also in stone (unlike others in the region which, lacking time or resources, had to make-do with temporary sheds of wood). Gracious balustrades on either side crown the cornice.

The church in Barcelona, finished after 1874, is the most complete stone building of the Spanish period in Sorsogon province

Steps leading to the tower on the façade

Ruins extending perpendicularly from the left side of the church may have been of an early convento. Across the atrium are ruins of the tribunal and school, which would have dramatically framed the church as one approached from the sea.

It is ironic that the architecture of Barcelona has been popularly ascribed to the Franciscans, when in fact Sorsogon province had been ceded by the Franciscans to the secular clergy of the diocese of Nueva Cáceres since 1794. Most of these diocesan priests were native Bicolanos. A handful of stone churches or sections of them built by the Spanish-era native priests, who were as capable as their Franciscan forbears, may still be seen in Bacon (a tower), Gubat, Bulan, Bulusan (a fortification), and Matnog.

The interior recently underwent a major renovation, with ceiling painting and a central altarpiece based chiefly on neoclassic motifs.

Parish Church of St. Ignatius of Loyola

Parish Church of
the Immaculate Conception
of Our Lady

Parish Church of St. Joseph

SECTION SEVEN: EASTERN VISAYAS

The islands of Samar and Leyte constitute the "backbone" of the Philippine archipelago. Confronting the Pacific, they received the galleons from Acapulco as well as the brunt of the monsoon typhoons, which occasionally washed ashore islanders from far-away Palao. The Jesuits inaugurated their mission here in 1595, with chapels in Carigara (Leyte) and Tinagon (now Dapdap, Samar). When they left in 1768, the Franciscans took over most of Samar, while the Augustinians were entrusted with Leyte and southeastern Samar. These latter areas were eventually turned over to the Franciscans, except for western Leyte, which became the enclave of the Seculars.

SECTION SEVEN: Eastern Visayas

Parish Church of St. Ignatius of Loyola

**Municipality of Capul, 6408
Northern Samar, Philippines
Feast day: July 31
Diocese of Catarman**

One has only to see the churning waves of the Pacific (blue) smash against those of the Philippines (brownish) at the northern tip of Capul island to get a hint of the challenges in negotiating these waters.

Yet historically the surging seas were culture channels. The islanders called their home Abag and continue speaking Inabaknon, which linguistically is most closely related to Yakan spoken in Basilan—which in turn suggests a pre-Hispanic link to Sulu and even Borneo. The Capuleños maintained farms in mainland Samar, and sometimes surpassed the towns here in population.

By 1600 the Jesuits had established a mission here. But because the island was a strategic stopover for the Manila galleons along the Embocadero (the passage between Luzon and Samar), Capul became a target for pirates. In 1642 Dutch corsairs burned the church, but when the aromatic flames betrayed it was of sandalwood, they carted the rest away. A fortified church of roughly hewn stone was commenced by the Jesuits around the second half of the 17th century. The Franciscans took over in 1768 and ministered here until 1898. Invited to return in 1907, the Franciscans served up to the 1920s.

The church bisects the fort. The façade of the church is very plain, except for the triangular pediment over the doorway which seems to have been interrupted by a window; or did the builder intend it without an apex? The quadrangular belltower standing apart is remarkable for its mass, which dominates the frontage. The original pyramidal roof has recently been restored.

Constructed around the second half of the 17th century, the fortified church of Capul replaced an earlier one of sandalwood. Until the late 19th century, the only way inside the enclosure was through the church's façade.

Carved wooden image of San Ignacio de Loyola, patron of Capul

The interior of the church is rather bare, witness to the typhoons that have ravaged the site. The retablo is a modern reconstruction, but the original red tile flooring is preserved. An image of San Ignacio de Loyola, in black cassock, and another of San Francisco de Asís, caped in brown, symbolize the two religious orders that ministered (and defended) this lonely outpost.

The fort is quadrangular in plan, with bastions at each corner. The two facing the sea (eastwards) are circular—a cannon still commands the northeast—while the two facing inland (westwards) are like aces of spades. The crenellations crowning the walls recall European castles, but are unique in the Philippines. On either side of the church is an open field where the populace under siege took refuge.

The colonial-style retablo recently replaced a rather modernist altarpiece.

Parish Church of the Immaculate Conception of Our Lady

Church Road, Guiuan, 6809
Eastern Samar, Philippines
Feast day: December 8
Diocese of Borongan

The Jesuits, operating from across the gulf in Dulag, Leyte opened a mission in Guiuan in 1595. Increasing pirate raids led to the raising of a quadrangular fort that by about the mid-1600s was the third largest in the country, after Manila and Zamboanga. The Augustinians took over from the Jesuits in 1768, and ministered until 1795. The Franciscans arrived in 1804. They erected a transept (1840s-1850s), a baptistry, a belltower over the southern bastion (1854), two schools, and even a pier.

The present church of cut coralstone was constructed between 1718 and 1740; it is fortified by steeply inclined step buttresses. Like the one in Capul, it bisects the fort into two open spaces; the entrance to the fort until the 19th century was through its façade. From the Jesuit era are the gorgeously carved baroque doors on the main and side entrances and the images flanking the main entrance (San Ignacio Loyola upholding a chalice and host, and San Luis Gonzaga cradling the Christ Child).

The Jesuits built the present church to replace one that burned down in 1718, which itself stood on the site of earlier ones built in the 1630s and 1660s. Native wealth, brought by trade in slaves, gold, and coconut oil, necessitated a fortification that incorporated the church in the mid-1600s.

Intricate shellwork mosaic in the baptistry

The retablos in the sanctuary and the left transept are also from the Jesuit period. The Augustinian presence is attested to by a rococo panel fronting the right side retablo. The Franciscans introduced a unique decorative scheme: mosaics of 106 species of shells and corals accenting cornices and pilasters, culminating in the baptistry.

Magellan made his first Philippine landfall in 1521 in Homonhon, an island just south of Guiuan.

Thanks to its being on the eastern-most edge of the Visayas, facing the Pacific, Guiuan has had more than its share of international relations. Its name is likely derived from *gigwanum*, a source of salty water (such is the water in the town today).

In the 17th century, the inhabitants through inter-island trading in coconut oil were among the wealthiest in the region. In 1696 twenty-nine Palau islanders were cast ashore at Guiuan, a clue to ancient navigation routes. In 1944 the Americans built a huge naval complex on the surrounding islands from which they staged the liberation of Leyte, thus commencing the wresting of the country from the Japanese. These war-time facilities were rehabilitated as a transit point for the White Russian refugees, from 1949 to 1951.

On the left-hand side of the church stands a monument to Donato Guimbaolibot, native patriot and parish priest of nearby Balangiga when enraged townsfolk attacked the American camp in 1901. The famous bells were then sequestered and returned only in 2018.

The central retablo is the most baroque altarpiece in the eastern Visayas. Images of Jesuit saints were replaced with those of the Franciscans in the early 1800s.

Parish Church of St. Joseph

Brgy. San Isidro, Matalom, 6526
Leyte, Philippines
Feast day: May 27
Diocese of Maasin

The early evangelization of western Leyte was due to the Jesuits, with centers in Ormoc, Palompon, Baybay, Hilongos, and Maasin. After 1768 these passed on to the Augustinians. By 1806 they were all administered by the diocesan clergy, who built the stone churches in Baybay, Matalom, and San Juan (Cabalian).

The oldest part of the church in Matalom is the apse. Its solid rubblework construction and pairs of narrow rectangular windows liken it to a bulwark. It is almost a twin of the San Carlos blockhouse in adjacent Maasin, which is dated 1771, and most possibly was part of that town's defense system against slave raids. When these threats had passed, the Matalom *baluarte* was converted into the residence of the missionary, and a balcony surrounding the upper level was built (of which only a few beams remain).

Today's church of cut stone was eventually attached to the *baluarte*. An inscription nearby, "*cemintu sa 1832*" suggests that construction began even before it was declared a parish independent of Hilongos in 1861.

Towards the apex of the façade are the papal tiara and crossed keys of St. Peter, signifying that the church was administered by the diocesan clergy. The façade follows the revival of classical or renaissance prototypes of the day, such as Vignola's original design for Il Gesú in Rome. Over the portico are a dark-skinned St. Joseph and Child. Several roof-tiles are still in place.

The church in Matalom developed in the 1830s as an extension of a 1770s blockhouse, which now serves as its apse and sacristy. To the right is a likeness of Father Leonardo Celes Díaz, first parish priest and builder not just of this church but of the tower in Hilongos.

A bird in flight on a lamp holder

A monument in front of the church commemorates Padre Leonardo Celes (spelled Cells in other records) Díaz as the builder of the church and its first parish priest. The dates cited for his tenure, 1843-1883, overlap with his being parish priest of Hilongos from about 1840 to 1861 (he was simultaneously vicar forane for the western coast of Leyte). It may be that while at Hilongos (where he built the belltower) he was also attending to the growing faith community in Matalom.

The belltower, interestingly, was built separate from the church; a curtain wall connects it with the façade. The interior of the ground level is completely faced with cut stone (unexpected for this type of space); in fact a complete altar has been incorporated within one of the four gigantic arches that constitute this chamber. The upper levels of concrete were added in later times.

The central retablo is modern, but the wooden communion rail, pulpit, eagle-shaped lamp holders and confessionals are still extant.

Though the original retablo has disappeared, the image of Saint Joseph and the communion rail date from the 19th century. The floor of wood was later replaced with tiles.

Parish Church of the
Immaculate Conception of Our Lady

Minor Basilica of the Holy Child
(Santo Niño)

Parish Church of the
Patronage of Mary
(Patrocinio de Maria)

Parish Church of the
Immaculate Conception
of Our Lady

Parish Church of
St. Augustine of Hippo

Parish Church of St. Isidore the Farmer

SECTION EIGHT: CENTRAL VISAYAS

The islands of Cebu, Bohol, and Siquijor, and the southeastern half of Negros Island, are united culturally by the Cebuano language, or Sugbuhanon in the vernacular. In the city of Cebu, which became the seat of the eponymous diocese in 1595, were located the central houses of the religious orders working in the Visayas: those of the Augustinians (1565), the Jesuits (1595), and the Augustinian Recollects (1622).

The Augustinians administered southeastern Cebu. The Jesuits worked in Bohol from 1596 until 1768. The Seculars were active in western Cebu. The Recollects took over Bohol after 1768 and Negros in the mid-19th century.

Minor Basilica of the Holy Child (Santo Niño)

**Osmeña Boulevard, Cebu City, 6000
Cebu, Philippines
Feast day: Third Sunday of January
Archdiocese of Cebu**

The Minor Basilica of the Santo Niño stands on the site where an 11-inch wooden statuette of the Child Jesus was discovered on 28 April 1565. This Santo Niño is generally believed to be the same one given by Magellan to Raja Humabon's wife on 14 April 1521, and is thus considered the oldest Christian icon in the Philippines.

The provisional church that the Augustinians built was the first such edifice in the islands. It was replaced by a brick one that had to be demolished in the 1730s. Father Juan Albarrán directed the construction of the present church. From his experience, he prepared a manual, "Admonitions for projects that this convento may undertake," which is kept in the Archivo de la Provincia de Agustinos Filipinos in Valladolid, Spain. He advocated the use of *manunggul* (now called "Mactan") stone which could be easily cut and transported. Albarrán's system of rafters and secondary rafters was implemented in Boljoon and other churches.

The main entrance steps are flanked by Chinese lions, which also top newel posts in the stairway to the convento, completed around 1760. For the hexagonal belltower (reconstructed after the 2013 earthquake), seven bells were destined, dating from 1750 (dedicated to the Santo Niño) to 1930.

The façade and tower of the church of the Santo Niño, built from 1735 to 1740, became the model for other churches in Cebu such as Opon and San Nicolás. The triangular finials supporting circles were copied in Argao (1788), Boljoon (1789), and Dalaguete also in Cebu.

The image of the Santo Niño, of the type made in early 16th century Mechelen, Belgium, is of a boy standing, holding a globe in his left hand and raising two fingers of his right hand in blessing. When found in 1565, a red velvet bonnet was on his head, and there were signs of wear on his cheek. The natives told the Spaniards that during a drought they would wade into the sea ("*sugbô*") with the image and successfully "persuade" him to let the rains fall.

Centuries later in his bulletproof altar, he wears breeches, a golden crown, boots, and a military commander's staff. Public devotion to the Santo Niño antedates by more than half a century that of the Holy Infant of Prague—who is distinguished from his Cebuano counterpart by his long gown—because the Czech image was only enshrined in the Carmelite church there in 1628.

Devotees dance the *sinulog*—which occasionally was performed in the church—and leave toys behind.

The sumptuously carved central retablo, dating from the 1740s, is arguably the widest in the Philippines.

GOZOS DEL SANTO NIÑO DE CEBU

Batobalani sa gugma, sa daan tao palangga.
Coro: Canamo malooy ca unta nǧa canimo nanǧilaba.

Ang sa Sogbong pagcadunggo, sa mǧa cachilang tao,
dinhi hinpalgan icao sa usa canilang sundalo,
cay caniya icao napaquita, guican lamang sa imong gugma. (Coro)

Ang balay nǧa hinpalgan sa imo nǧa catahuman
nahimo nǧa catilingban sa mǧa taong daghanan,
ang nǧatanan naninǧalal cay guionhan mo man sila. (Coro)

Guisimba icao ug guiludhan ni Legazpi nǧa punuan,
cay icao niya ang hingquitan sa iyang paghidalagan,
sa maragaang nǧa gugma nagamatuod nǧa Dios cang bata. (Coro)

Cadtong mǧa taong daghan ang gugma nila guiasdang
sa pagbuhat ug simbahan sa canimo nǧa hipalgan,
nǧa guipanaghalad nila canimo Dios sa higugma. (Coro)

Ang imong mǧa catahuman sa among calag calipayan,
sa among saquit inǧon tambal, ug sa among cahanǧul manggad,
sa nǧatanan quinahanglan icao ang among dalangpan. (Coro)

Icao lamang ang ampo-on sa mga daang sugbuanon
nǧa canimo nanagbaton cun naay quinahanglanon,
busa guinǧanlan ca nila alampo-on balahala. (Coro)

Cun olan ang panǧayoon ug imong pagadugayon,
Dada-on ca sa baybayon ug sa dagat pasalomon,
ug dayon nila macuha ang olan nǧa guitinǧuha. (Coro)

Icao gayod ang tuburan ning lonlon catinǧalahan,
busa icao guilohoan niining mǧa capopodan,
Pagton-an mo ang sacop nila sa matarong nǧa higugma. (Coro)

Icao ang among guisaligan malig-on ug matuod nǧa dalangpán
sa among mǧa quinahanglan, cay diosnon cang mananabang,
ipaquita ang imong gugma oh lanǧitnon Bálahala. (Coro)

Bato balani sa gugma sa daan tao palangga.
Canamo malooy ca unta nǧa canimo nanǧilaba.

From: *Novena ug pagdayeg sa Santísimo Niño Jesús
nga guisingba sa Ciudad sa Sugbu.* [1888]
Biblioteca Nacional de España, R 33.321/37.

JOYS OF THE HOLY CHILD OF CEBU

Magnet of love, beloved by the people from of old.
Refrain: - Have mercy on us, we implore you.

You were brought to Cebu by the Spaniards;
here you were found by one of their soldiers,
for you appeared before him, out of your love. (Ref.)

The home, where you were found in your glory,
has become a thriving community-
awed, because you foreshadowed them. (Ref.)

The herald Legazpi knelt and worshiped you,
for he discovered you in his voyage;
in your tender love, you manifest yourself as the God who
became a child. (Ref.)

The community's love dared
to construct the church where you were found-
they now offer this to you, the God of love. (Ref.)

Your manifold radiance in our soul makes us joyful,
in our sickness you are our remedy, and in our greed, you are our
treasure, for in all our needs, you are our refuge. (Ref.)

You are the only one worshipped by the Cebuanos of old;
to you they come bearing their need,
so they named you their adored Deity. (Ref.)

If they ask for rain and this you delay,
they will take you to the shore and have you swim in the sea
and promptly they obtain the rain they ask for. (Ref.)

Verily you are the wellspring of pure wonderment,
and so you are adored in these islands;
teach then their inhabitants honorable love. (Ref.)

You are the one we trust, strong and true refuge
of our needs, for you are the Divine Helper.
Show us your love, o heavenly Deity. (Ref.)

Magnet of love, beloved by the people of old.
- Have mercy on us, we implore you.

The Santo Niño, oldest image of Christ in the Philippines

Parish Church of the Patronage of Mary (Patrocinio de Maria)

Boljoon, 6024
Cebu, Philippines
Feast day: Second Saturday of November
Archdiocese of Cebu

Nestled in a small cove and guarded by the steep Ili hill, Boljoon was nourished by streams ("*bolho*" in Visayan) that may have given it its name. The Augustinians planted their mission cross here as early as 1599. Excavations in the churchyard begun in 2007 unearthed burials with iron daggers, gold necklaces and early 17th century Chinese and Japanese plates. Except for a brief Jesuit interlude (1737-1747), Boljoon remained an Augustinian ministry until 1948. It was the southeasternmost bastion of Spanish Cebu for two centuries, until the separation of Oslob in the 1830s.

The church complex bisects the narrow strip of land between the sea and the hills, so that the populace could rush in from north or south to seek refuge during a pirate raid.

In the devastating attack of 1782, the church was burned. Apparently, the stone edifice was already being constructed, as may be theorized by the survival of certain altarpieces. Inscriptions on the stones date the left and right side entrances to 1789, and the façade to 1801.

This façade is based on ratios of squares and triangles, marked by pilasters emblazoned with ribbon-like belts that symbolize the Augustinians' Rule given by Our Lady of Consolation. The image of the patroness, "The Patronage of Our Lady," is ensconced in an *urna* or domestic altar. Below her are the Augustinian saints Nicolás de Tolentino and Juan de Sahagún.

A geometrically proportioned façade was applied in 1801 on the church which had been standing for at least two decades earlier.

Carved newel post in the convento

During his first tenure as parish priest (1802-1827), Father Julian Bermejo fortified the compound with a stone wall, erected a blockhouse on its south-eastern corner, and put up a signal tower on Ili hill. He established a defense system linking southeastern Cebu (96 kilometers of bulwarks and towers) with the surrounding islands. He even assisted in the pacification of the Dagohoy Revolt in Bohol in 1827. Within his later terms (1829-1837, 1839-1842, and 1846-1848), he concluded the church's transept (1829) and convento (1841), and promoted local industries such as the weaving of *patadyong* tube-skirts.

The interior is an unforgettable treasury of two centuries of art. The three baroque retablos, stylistically from the middle of the 18th century, possibly survived the 1782 fire. Archival evidence provides dates for certain pieces: the frontals of the side retablos (1798), the pulpit (1807; the panels of bishop-saints "disappeared one stormy night"), the pipe organ (1870s), and the altarpieces by the transept (1910). The pierced screen of the choir loft is carved on *both* sides.

The exuberant baroque style of the central retablo antedates the rebuilding of the church in the 1780s, and thus may have pertained to an earlier edifice.

Parish Church of the Immaculate Conception of Our Lady

Población, Báclayon, 6301
Bohol, Philippines
Feast day: December 8
Diocese of Tagbilaran

The Jesuits took over their first Bohol mission in Báclayon in 1596, upon the request of the mother of the Spanish administrator of the island. Its tranquility behind a mangrove swamp (which protected the village from storm surges) was deceptive. Thirty years earlier, Portuguese and Ternatans disguised as Spaniards pillaged the place, leaving only stumps where houses stood over the water. (Centuries later, even the beach disappeared when unscrupulous agents ferried off the sand to resorts in other islands.)

According to Jesuit scholars, the present church of cut coralstone dates from 1727. The base of a tower and a bulwark date from about the same period. The Augustinian Recollects who took over in 1768 enlarged the fortifications and finished the tower in 1777. Throughout the second half of the 19th century, they added a baptistry (1850), a mortuary chapel (1859), a convento (1872), and a portico over the old façade (1875).

For the community, they built two schools, some bridges, and even the market across the convento. The church and tower were damaged during the earthquake of 2013, but were eventually restored.

The triple-arched façade was added in 1875 by the Augustinian Recollects as an extension from the earlier one built by the Jesuits in about 1727. Similarly, the bulk of the belltower was completed by the former in 1777, on a base laid by the latter.

Kyrie of the 1827 *Misa Baclayana*

The retablo in the sanctuary and the two flanking it are from the first half of the 18th century, and are among the best examples of Philippine baroque. The decoration on the image of the patroness in the central niche, the Immaculate Conception, is a rare example of a technique simulating thick embroidery.

The two other side retablos, most of the statuary, and the pulpit are of 19th century vintage. Projecting over the right side is the *tribuna*, a balcony where priests could contemplate the tabernacle from the upper convento.

Over the choir loft is a pipe organ, constructed under the aegis of Diego Cera, the famous builder of the "Bamboo Organ" in Las Piñas (both instruments date from 1824). The expertise gained in Báclayon led to the building between 1830 and 1850 of pipe organs in other Bohol churches: Dímiao, Loáy, Lóboc, and Loón. Church music that was vibrant in Bohol is exemplified by *cantoral* manuscripts in the museum, where the *Misa Baclayana* (1827) is displayed. San Blas, patron of the throat, is represented in the retablo left of the sanctuary.

The four corners of the campanile support faces that presumably kept watch over all directions. Their extended ears and *santol* fruit-shaped heads recall pre-Hispanic earthenware portraiture, just like those on the tower of Dauis across the strait.

The central retablo is one of the most iconic of Philippine baroque. Apart from the patronal image in the center of lowest tier, which dates from the Jesuit era, the other statues were installed here between 1810 and 1875.

Parish Church of the Immaculate Conception of Our Lady

Bohol Circumferential Road, Duero, 6309
Bohol, Philippines
Feast day: December 8
Diocese of Talibón

The town of Duero was founded in 1862 by joining parts of Jagna to the west and Guindulman to the east. It was named after a river which traverses Spain and Portugal. The Augustinian Recollects ministered here until 1898, and then resumed until the 1930s.

The present church was commenced in the 1860s and blessed in 1874. It is a mostly wooden interpretation of the Greek Revival popular in the second half of the 19th century and after, when churches, banks and houses emulated Greek temples. A clearly delineated triangular pediment, fluted columns, and a Doric frieze that runs all along the upper reaches of the walls, are typical elements of the style. The shady portico before the main entrance is a feature of many churches in Bohol and Cebu, propagated first by the Augustinian Recollects from the 1860s onwards, and still in favor way into the 20th century.

Duero's unprepossessing frontage masks interesting details. (Do not judge a church by its façade, to paraphrase.) The "fluted" columns are actually tree trunks encased in wood panels, with alternating lumber strips that simulate the fluting. The triangle with the eye of God on the pediment might look like a Masonic symbol to some, but is actually an important Christian icon. The clouds surrounding the eye are outlined with a double line, a typical Oriental touch.

The church of Duero, inaugurated in 1874, is an artfully crafted wood interpretation of a Greek temple—a style that became popular in the Philippines in the latter half of the nineteenth century.

Triune eye of God in a pediment sunburst

The interior from floor to trusses is of wood, with an acoustic that is perfect for *a capella* singing. Well-polished floorboards of dark *bayong* alternate with light *tugas* hardwood, rivaled only by the parquetry in Valencia a few towns to the west. The ceiling is completely paneled in wood, among the most intact of its kind in the country. Its *artesonado* or coffered design has recently been renewed, simulating a three-dimensional effect.

The church's skeletal framework consists of sturdy posts, with a low *cota* or rubblework wall between them. Over the *cota*, wooden panels were laid horizontally for the exterior, while they were erected vertically for the interior. The religious complex escaped the burning of the town by American forces during the Philippine-American War in 1901 (the towns of Batuanan—now Alicia, Sierra Bullones, and Sevilla were not as lucky; they were so scourged they had to be relocated).

In 1919, for further protection, the outside walls were sheathed with zinc sheets bearing the logo of Wolverhampton, an English industrial city, and the Australian emu.

The severe, straight lines of the Greek façade are softened in the central retablo with leafy swags and borders.

Parish Church of St. Augustine of Hippo

Población, Bacong, 6216
Negros Oriental, Philippines
Feast day: August 28
Diocese of Dumaguete

The Augustinians established a mission in 1580 in Tanjay, a shore-line community in Negros (known then as Isla de Buglas) dominated by the crater of Mount Talinis. One of the *visitas* was Marabago, the future Bacong. The mission was soon ceded to the Seculars. In 1846, Bacong—named after a local plant similar to the spider lily—was separated ecclesiastically from Dumaguete. It received its first Augustinian Recollect parish priest in 1849.

The present church was begun in 1866 during Father Leandro Arrué's first term (1864-1868). A foreman was contracted to select lumber and direct the weekly shift of workers. Some of the wood for the floorboards was cut in Tanjay, about 44 kilometers to the north, while other timber was felled in Bais, a bit further at about 58 kilometers. The edifice with walls of bricks on a footing of cut stone was blessed on the feast day of San Agustín in 1883 by Father Arrué on his second term (1882-1885).

The foundations for the belltower were laid by Father Arrué, but it was concluded only in the 1890s. The precise fitting of irregularly angled stone blocks is arguably the best in the country. The arrangement of steps around a massive tree trunk leading to the top is another unique and rare feature.

The construction in the 1880s of the church in Bacong was so well-managed that it was a positive factor in the appointment of its builder, Father Leandro Arrué, as bishop of Jaro.

The only Spanish-period pipe organ in Negros

The neoclassic retablos were complemented with other furnishing acquired earlier. Those that are still extant include the image of the patron San Agustín (acquired from Siquijor in 1848); the *cajonería* or vestment chest in the sacristy (from Dumaguete, 1849); the tabernacle and *gradillas* (risers for candles and flower vases), candlestands, an *andas* or processional platform with handle-bars (now mounted on wheels), and an image of the Resurrected Christ (all of wood and acquired in 1850); a large image of the Crucified Christ (1851); and the archives cabinet (1864).

The convento, which was built from 1854 to 1860, was also rehabilitated in the early 1880s. This building has a well-preserved *aljibe* (cistern) over which is the *azotea* (terrace).

Father Arrué's term was cut when he was appointed bishop of Jaro in 1885. He gifted his beloved parish with his portrait in bishop's robes, which now hangs in the convento.

The pipe organ, imported from the Roqués company in Zaragoza, Spain, was installed in 1894. Thirty-nine of its 581 pipes are wood.

The Augustinian Recollects returned to Bacong in 1904, and entrusted it to the diocese in 1965.

The majestic, neoclassic proportions of the retablo provide a meaningful frame for the patron saint, Saint Augustine, whose writings introduced classical thought into Christian philosophy.

Parish Church of St. Isidore the Farmer

Catamboan, Población, Lazi, 6228
Siquijor, Philippines
Feast day: May 15
Diocese of Dumaguete

The ministry of Siquijor on the eponymous island was entrusted by the Seculars to the Augustinian Recollects in 1794. The *visita* of Lazi was separated as an independent parish in 1857. The town derives its curious name from Manuel Pavía y Lacy, Philippine governor general for only nine months in 1854, during which time Siquijor was separated from the civil administration of Cebu and annexed to Bohol. The church complex was erected on the edge of a plateu called Tigbawan, the town's earlier name taken from the abundant *tigbao* grass (known elsewhere as *talahib*).

The present church and convento took shape during the administration of Father Toribio Sánchez (1882-1894). Fray Toribio brought with him experience from improving the church (now cathedral) in Romblon, his previous assignment. In Lazi, he concluded both church and convent. Most of the cruciform church's walls is of rough coralstone rubblework, plastered with lime. In contrast, cut coralstone blocks were applied over the façade, dated 1884 over the main doorway, and the belltower, dated 1885. A corner of the belltower is carved with the names of Don Alberto Buncavel, *gobernadorcillo* (mayor) of the town, and Don Valentín Baroro, director of the project. Father Sánchez chose not to be mentioned. Flanking the main entrance are pedestals for the fluted pilasters that feature chiseled out cartwheel-like ornaments. In between the pedestals and pilasters, the stonecutters incised blocks with vegetal designs.

Wood is also very visible. Wooden planks form the pediments of all four frontages of the church. A wooden statue of an unidentified female saint is atop the cupola.

Cut coralstone blocks (topped by a pediment of wooden planks) mask the 1884 façade, which like most of the church was built of rubblework.

The neoclassic retablos and the twin pulpits (for both epistle and gospel readings) are made of wood. Most especially, alternating light-and-dark floorboards form a fishbone design on the nave, and the more intricate pattern of trapezoids in the baptistry.

The largest convento in the Philippines?

Across the street Fray Toribio built a residence where, as he explained, sick priests could recuperate. The convento—arguably the largest in the country—is a gigantic *balay nga bato* (colonial stone house). The dining room adjoined a wide terrace that concealed a two-compartment cistern where rainwater was collected. Another passage led to the separately built kitchen, under which were kept livestock and poultry. The edifice has conserved its *tabique pampango* (interwoven bamboo slats) partitions, *amakan* (plaited bamboo strip mat) ceilings, and costly colored glass windowpanes. Lazi was—and is—indeed well-placed to receive travelers from the surrounding islands of Negros, Cebu, Bohol, Camiguin and northern Mindanao.

The three pediments of the central retablo are each emblazoned with symbols of the sun, an unusual allusion to the Holy Trinity.

Cathedral of St. Joseph

Parish Church of St. Mónica

Parish Church of St. John of Nepomuk
(San Juan Nepomuceno)

Parish Church of St. Joseph the Worker

Parish Church of St. Thomas of Villanova
(Santo Tomas de Villanueva)

SECTION NINE: WESTERN VISAYAS

The formal evangelization of Western Visayas began with the establishment of Augustinian missions in 1572 in Oton and Pan-ay, both on the island which took its name from the latter town. This apostolate was then extended among the Hiligaynon-, Karay-a-, and Aklanon-speaking communities in the rest of Panay.

The Augustinian Recollects ministered in Romblon and western Negros, lands which were incorporated with the diocese of Jaro upon its establishment in 1865. The Seculars and Jesuits also held parishes in several parts of Panay and Negros. The Mill Hill Fathers continued the work of the friars, from 1908 to the present.

PARISH CHURCH OF
ST. ISIDORE THE FARMER

Vicmico, Victorias City, 6119
Negros Occidental, Philippines
Feast day: May 1
Diocese of Bacolod

Right after the ravages of World War II, Miguel J. Ossorio planned a community that would reflect the social teachings of the Church in his vast sugar central at Victorias. His son Frederic Ossorio y Yangco—one of the original Monuments Men, who retrieved a Van Gogh from an Austrian salt mine—returned from war service in Europe and forthwith contacted Raymond and Rado of New York to design an earthquake-proof church. Czech-American Antonin Raymond had worked with Frank Lloyd Wright in Tokyo, where he developed his earthquake-resistant designs after the 1923 temblor. His model for Victorias appeared in the November 1947 issue of *Liturgical Arts*. (It's been said that Frederic was introduced to a provincemate, Leandro Locsin, who prepared a round church plan, but actually Locsin hadn't finished his studies at this time.)

The church was made of locally manufactured concrete blocks. It consisted of two interlocking structures on separate foundations: a nave with a low façade, and a skeletal tower over the sanctuary. Light and fresh air flowed through the pierced walls and numerous openings. The artworks were finished in 1950.

The completion of the church in the Victorias sugar central in 1949 introduced modern church architecture in the country. It was conceived not only to resist earthquake but also – with its unprepossessing façade – to visualize the Church's teachings on social reform.

Benjamin Valenciano's *Pinoy* Christ

Frederic's brother Alfonso, an accomplished artist and patron of abstractionists like Pollock and Dubuffet, came from his studio in the U.S. and worked on the murals. His livid colors were fixed on cement with a new and rarely used binder. He depicted God's love, through the Sacred Heart, to figure prominently as the early morning sun lit up the celebrant.

Almost all the human figures were portrayed as identifiably dark-skinned and local. Adé de Bethune, a Belgian-American liturgical artist and colleague of the Catholic activist Dorothy Day, fitted broken pieces of bottles into mosaics featuring the life of Saint Joseph. Mary, Joseph, and a clean-shaven Crucified Christ were carved by Benjamin Valenciano, a migrant carpenter from Manila. He also depicted Pilate and the soldiers in the Stations of the Cross as military men in boots. The brass cutouts of the lecterns and baptismal font were crafted by Arcadio Anore.

Pursuing their dream to make Negros "the Capital of Catholic Social Action," the Ossorios invited the Salesians of Don Bosco to set up a school for the children of employees and workers. The technical institute they opened in 1951 was their first in the Philippines.

Ossorio interpreted God's love as a "continual Last Judgment:" not as "The Angry Christ."

Parish Church of St. Thomas of Villanova (Santo Tomas de Villanueva)

Miag-ao, 5023
Iloilo, Philippines
Feast day: September 22
Archdiocese of Jaro

After pirate attacks in 1741 and 1754, the people of Miag-ao and their Augustinian pastor moved to a hill overlooking the sea and an eponymous river (named, they say, after the *miagos* or *mayagos* plant then abundant in the area). There, bolstered by earnings from the town's busy looms, they embarked on building a church capacious enough to accommodate the populace during a raid, and stable enough to withstand earthquakes. According to local tradition, work was directed by a foreman named Matias from nearby Igbaras; later, he was succeeded by Aquino from Alimodian. The construction of this yellow-orange limestone fortress baroque church lasted from 1786 to 1797.

The stone carvers applied their own esthetics in the selection, layout and distribution of motifs copied from books. Doric and rococo counterpoint each other in a lithic symphony scored on the façade, towers, and walls: a *crescendo* here, an *agitato* there. On the pediment, a burly Saint Christopher with rolled-up pants supports the Christ Child; he clutches a coconut palm—the Filipino tree of life—and is surrounded by fruit-heavy papaya and guava trees. Ensconced in a niche of fluttering C-scrolls is the patron saint, Thomas of Villanova, archbishop of Valencia, shown giving alms to the needy. (The original stone image is in the vestibule of the church.)

On the façade of the church of Miag-ao, built from 1786 to 1797, a fully resplendent coconut palm takes the role of a sunburst. The tower on the left scoured the sea for pirate attacks, while the one on the right rose only in 1830.

Side window with rocalla-style C-scroll "ears"

Instead of the usual statues of Saints Peter and Paul (apostles to the Jews and Gentiles) flanking the doorway, the builders chose to depict the Union of Church and State. These institutions were represented, respectively on the right by Saint Peter (the seal is that of Pope John XXIII, on whose last year—1963—the marker of the Philippine Historical Committee was installed), and on the left, by Saint Ferdinand III of Castile and the royal arms of Castile and Leon. Saint Ferdinand—the only canonized Spanish king—may also have added moral support, having fought the Moors.

Not to be missed are the frothy carved windows lining the exterior of the nave (two of which have been turned into doorways). Atop the window on the right tower (which illumines the baptistry), an eagle spreads its wings, while a cherub peers from the side.

The church was burned twice—in 1898 during the revolution against Spain, and then a few years later in the war against the Americans—which is why the interior is completely new.

Today's quasi-baroque retablo replaced the one lost in the 1898 fire.

Parish Church of St. John of Nepomuk (San Juan Nepomuceno)

Anini-y, 5717
Antique, Philippines
Feast day: May 16
Diocese of San Jose de Antique

Augustinian missionary attempts in what is now the province of Antique were largely tentative for the first two centuries due to pirate attacks, difficulty of access, and lack of personnel. Anini-y (its name possibly derived from a local word for a stream) was taken care of by the secular clergy from 1795 to 1875. Around 1818, Father Evangelista Magbanua erected a palisade at his own expense to defend the town against pirates. Due to its isolation Anini-y seems to have been bypassed by four rebellions that shook the province in 1828, 1834, the mid-1840s, and 1888.

The church complex is located by the sea, in a tranquil setting of verdant trees and shrubs—a welcome sight and happy surprise to any traveler. The façade, belltower and a section of the exterior walls are faced with cut coralstone, as well as the pilasters and window openings. The rest of the exterior walls, and that of the sanctuary, are of rubblework. Despite their unfinished state, the walls have weathered well, indicating the mastery of masonry that had been attained by the end of the 19th century.

Construction of the present church was begun by the Augustinian Jerónimo Vaquerín in 1875 but it was not quite finished when he left in 1898. There were no Catholic priests until the arrival of the Mill Hill Missionaries from England in 1908. Under their aegis, especially under Father William Erinkveld in the 1970s, the church has been well-maintained with great respect for the original building materials.

Begun in 1875, the church of Anini-y was left unfinished due to the revolution of 1898. The façade and tower are faced with cut and carved coralstone, but the rest of the rubblework walls have remained bare.

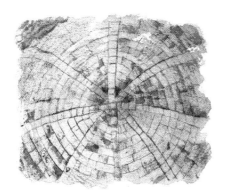

Masterly cut coralstone cupola of the belltower

The undercutting and distribution of the floral ornamentation on the arches over the main entrance and niches, as well as on the cornices and capitals of the pilasters, are of a refinement shared with the churches in San Joaquin and Guimbal across the mountains in Iloilo. The retablos in the sanctuary, side altars, and baptistry are also of stone, assembled in the neoclassic style. Curiously, what would ordinarily be a retablo pediment is a lunette shaped like an open fan or stylized *anahaw* leaf, not unlike the headgear of the Ati-atihan festival revelers in Aklan. The checker-board tiles are of a material meant to be gentle to bare feet. The solid rock baptismal font is one of the rare survivals in the whole of Panay Island.

But the precisely-cut stonework for the dome of the second level of the belltower is almost never noticed—except by Him who creates artists!

A modern altarpiece partially obscures the fan-shaped pediment of the original masonry retablo.

Parish Church of St. Mónica

Pan-ay, 5801
Capiz, Philippines
Feast day: August 27
Archdiocese of Capiz

Sitting on the delta of the Panay River, the community of Pan-ay was the site in 1569 of the Augustinians' first mission on the island that would eventually adapt its name. A late 17th century church was replaced by another of coralstone in the 1770s. After a typhoon in 1875, the edifice was reconstructed by Father José Beloso in 1884 (by then he had been parish priest for forty years).

A possible remnant of the older structure is the buttressed ruin behind the massive belltower. The side entrances have an inner, lower lintel, which even suggest that the earlier walls were "sandwiched" by the bigger church. The finials that resemble ornate rook chess pieces on the façade could also pertain to the 18th century edifice.

Ensconced in niches on the 1880s façade are coralstone images of San Agustín, Santo Tomás de Villanueva, and the patroness, Santa Mónica.

"I am the Voice of God," the largest bell in the country

The central retablo and the two across it at right angles are of the baroque of the first half of the 18th century. The main retablo seems too narrow for the width of the sanctuary, which suggests that it and the two others could have pertained to the earlier church. Each side retablo rests on a baseboard featuring angels blowing on flutes. The pediments recall the tumbling rococo C-scrolls on the Miag-ao façade, and could have been added at a later date over the slightly less quivering lower levels. (The side retablos have retained their original colors which should be conserved, in contrast with the central one whose polychrome was hidden by a silver finish.) The sanctuary is flanked by a pair of 19th century neoclassic retablos. Local historians credit the altarpieces to Joseph Bergaño or *Sarhento Itak,* although it is not clear in which period he lived. The roof is held up by a complex truss system; one of the enormous beams taken out of commission rests on one side of the nave.

Of the nine bells in the tower, seven were commissioned by Father Beloso from 1852 to 1885. The central bell, cast in 1878 by Juan Reina, is the largest in the country. 70 sacks of coins for the project were donated by the townsfolk; since silver is incompatible with bell metal, the cash probably paid for firewood and professional fees.

The Museum next to the church houses a rich collection of artifacts. Unfortunately, burglars some time ago made off with several treasures, among them a necklace with a baroque pearl.

The baroque central retablo is a remainder from the 18th century church.

Cathedral of St. Joseph

Población, Romblon 5500
Romblon, Philippines
Feast day: March 19;
also January, for the Santo Niño
Diocese of Romblon

Romblon and its surrounding islands have served a vital cultural link between the northern and southern parts of the Philippines since ancient times. A textile from minuscule Banton dates from about the 14th century.

The Augustinian Recollects were entrusted the ministry of Romblon from the diocesan clergy in 1635. Fray Agustín de San Pedro, *el padre capitán*, fortified the town and Banton in the mid-17th century. The islands weathered vicious pirate attacks throughout the 1700s. In the late 19th century, the carving of baptismal fonts from local marble made Romblon famous. After 1898 the Recollects were petitioned to return and served until the 1930s.

Foundations for the coralstone church and belltower date from about the 1650s. The rear of the church was securely set into the mountainside, a unique solution in the country. In the 1860s and 1870s, the walls were raised a few meters higher, which accounts for the façade being unusually tall in respect to its width, by Philippine standards. The original height may be gauged by the buttresses to the sides.

Zoom to the image of San José on the central niche to see the Christ Child affectionately tickling his earthly father's nape. The four-paneled main door (itself a rarity) is fully carved with 18th century floral ornaments. Other doors carry sun and fan motifs. The exterior walls were recently marred by an overlay of reticulated concrete, disrespecting the original layering of cut stone blocks.

Buttresses mark the height of the 1650s church of Romblon, which attained its present status in the 1870s. The brick level of the belltower, also begun in the 1650s, dates from 1727.

Disarming portrait of Saint Joseph on the façade, with the Baby Jesus

The elaborately carved central retablo bears the Roman numerals MDCCXXVI (1726), making it a benchmark for Philippine colonial art history. The three levels are topped by finials whose upturned coils remind one of the *kumintang* curled-fist movements of local dances. On both ends of the transept or "arms" of the church (constructed the same time the walls were elevated) are retablos with similar baroque elements. Contrasting with these are two neoclassic retablos flanking the sanctuary. The one on the left enshrines a Santo Niño given in 1728.

The ground level of the campanile, of solid stone, is said to be the headquarters of *el Padre Capitán*. The second is of alternating courses of stone and brick. The third is of brick, whose lime plaster has worn away, but the Roman numerals MDCCXXVII (1727) can still be discerned. The upper octagonal levels are of adobe. Visible from the church, Forts San Andrés and Santiago guard Romblon from opposite hills.

The central retablo, dated 1726, retains archaic strapwork ornaments on its base.

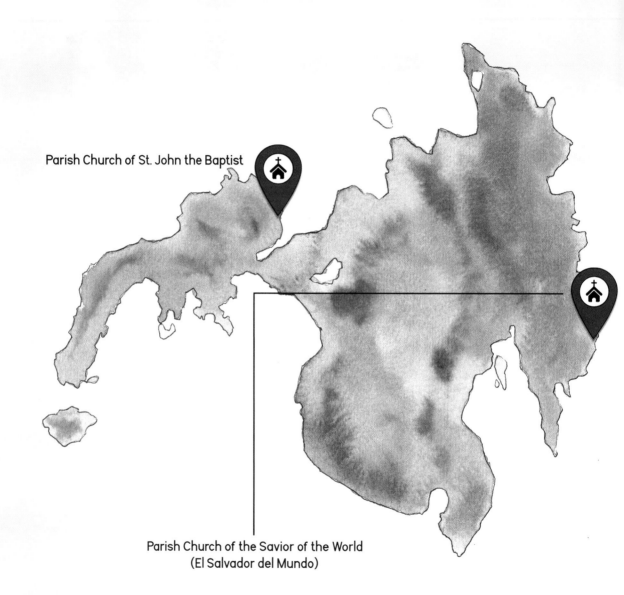

Parish Church of St. John the Baptist

Parish Church of the Savior of the World
(El Salvador del Mundo)

SECTION TEN: MINDANAO

In the Spanish period, the diverse cultural communities of Mindanao and nearby islands were evangelized principally by the Augustinian Recollects (Butuan, Cagayan, and Tandag, 1622; Davao, 1848; Isabela de Basilan, 1853) and the Jesuits (Dapitan, 1631, and Zamboanga, 1635; Tamontaka, Cotabato, 1862; a brick church was built in Jolo after 1875). The Benedictines were briefly in Surigao, 1895-1898. The Seculars filled in vacant posts.

After 1900, the Jesuits and Seculars were joined by other religious congregations with roots in Spain, Holland, Canada, France, the U.S.A., and other countries, who eventually reared local clergy and communities in the region with their particular charisms.

Parish Church of St. John the Baptist

Jimenéz, 7204
Misamis Occidental, Philipines
Feast day: June 24
Archdiocese of Ozamiz

The earlier name of Jimenéz was Palilan, a community along the eponymous river which originated from Mount Malindang and emptied into Iligan Bay. Originally closer to the sea, near the present-day oil depots, the community was transferred across the river to higher ground to avoid flooding. It adopted its present name to commemorate Father Francisco Jiménez, the Augustinian Recollect curate of Misamis (now Ozamiz City) who established the parish in 1859. The fledging community was composed of the indigenous Subanon (people of the *suba*, river) and Visayan settlers (mostly from Bohol).

The present church, of rubblework and cut coralstone cladding, was begun in the 1860s by its first parish priest, Father Roque Azcona (1862-1884). It is quite probable that the three-arched portico was intended to support a second level with a proper façade, as in Báclayon, Bohol (where the second level accommodates the storeroom behind the choir loft).

The church of Jimenéz, commenced in the 1860s and concluded in the 1880s, was restored in 1974 and in the early 2000s. It is the most completely preserved colonial religious edifice in Mindanao.

Rare example of clockwork, from the 1890s

Most of the interior was furnished in the late 1880s, including the neoclassic retablos with their silver fittings, the colored concrete floor tiles, choir loft, and stout pillars of *molave* (replacements of decayed nave supports). The central altarpiece is extraordinarily elaborate and colorful for its style. Separating the sanctuary from the sacristy are walls of *tabique pampango*— interwoven bamboo slats plastered with lime.

The walls and ceiling were painted in the 1890s by a young artist from Bilbao, Julio Sánz Cruzado. Surfaces of *tabique pampango* were made to look like cut stone. The clerestory (the section of the wall between the roof and the nave pillars) combines Doric triglyphs with paired Gothic arches. On the ceiling behind the central retablo and the sacristy, the earlier painting—stars and decorative bands—can still be seen. Tragically, the artist and his brother-in-law, Señor Ybarguen, were one of the few who perished in the Revolution.

The pipe organ from the Roqués company of Zaragoza, Spain was installed in 1894. Stored next to the instrument are large lanterns that figure in the Christmas Midnight mass, amid much music and singing. The Jimenez band singers, in fact, were considered the best in the province by the 1880s. The belltower with its clock and mechanism was completed in 1896.

The 1880s central retablo features a concave space for the patron San Juan Bautista and his parents San Zacarias and Santa Isabel (whose images are repeated on the portico).

Parish Church of the Savior of the World (El Salvador del Mundo)

Surigao-Davao Coastal Road, Población, Caraga, 8203
Davao Oriental, Philippines
Feast day: July 16
Diocese of Mati

A map dated 1659 first shows Caraga as the southernmost mission of the eponymous province that covered the entire eastern seaboard of Mindanao. The Augustinian Recollects ministered to Caraga from Bislig until a resident priest was assigned in 1804. A bell dated 1802 called the indigenous Mandaya to settle here. The first Jesuit priest, Pablo Pastells, took over in 1877. His assignment comprised most of what is today's Davao Oriental province.

Pastells initiated the construction of the church of rough coralstones, which was completed in 1884. Cut stones were used for the windows and corners, while the upper reaches were of wooden planks covered with lime plaster. It is the second oldest stone church in Mindanao, after Jimenez (1860s-1880s).

The Jesuits were succeeded in 1939 by the P.M.E. Fathers (Foreign Mission Society of Quebec), then by the Maryknoll Fathers in 1961; in 1986 the diocesan clergy took over. In 1995, when northeastern Mindanao was re-organized as the Caraga Region, Caraga was ironically left out as it remained within the Davao administrative region.

The late 19th century Caraga church retains the simple, squat silhouette of mission architecture.

Humble inscription on the façade with the Jesuit seal and year of completion

Inside the church, little remains of the original. Still authentic are the hewn hardwood pillars that march down the aisle to the sanctuary. Other pillars, not as straight, support the thick walls on both sides of the nave. The decayed old retablo was replaced by a modernistic one in the 1980s centennial rehabilitations. This in turn gave way to a more sympathetic altarpiece in the latest renovation.

In the central niche is the image of the church's dedicatee, El Salvador del Mundo. The iconography of Christ holding a globe in his hands is rarely encountered in the Spanish Philippines. However, this may be traced to the image's namesake, the provincial governor of Caraga, Don Salvador Ximénez Rendón, who personally gifted it to the church in 1805. Elsewhere in the retablo are images of San Ignacio de Loyola, founder of the Jesuits, and Our Lady of Mount Carmel, whose feast day (July 16) is the fiesta of Caraga.

The recent renovation of the church was inaugurated in July 2020. (It was also the time of the Covid-19 Pandemic, and in the unique event all celebrants and participants had to practice physical distancing and wear face masks.)

A short walk behind the church leads to a magnificent view of Caraga Bay. Across to the south is Pusan Point, the first part of the Philippines to greet the rising sun's rays.

The newly refurbished interior retained the original wood pillars.

FRONT COVER GUIDE

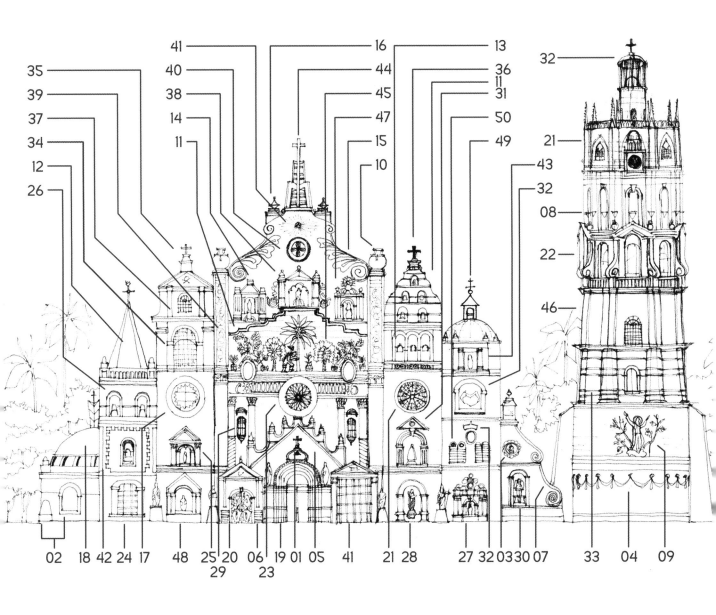

BACK COVER GUIDE

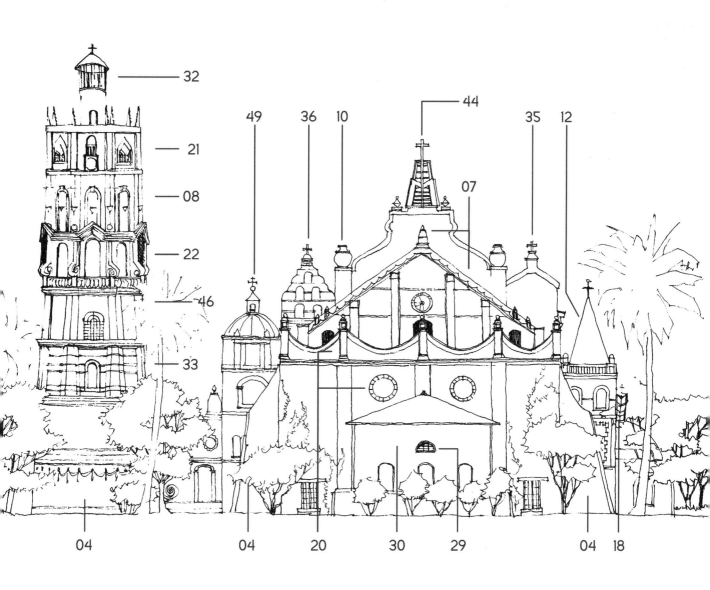

* Legend on next page

LEGEND FOR GUIDE MAP

1. Parish Church of St. Charles Borromeo
2. Parish Church of St. Raymund Peñafort
3. Parish Church of St. Paul the Hermit
4. Parish Church of St. Matthias
5. Parish Church of St. Vincent Ferrer
6. Parish Church of St. Mónica
7. Parish Church of St. Augustine
8. Metropolitan Cathedral of St. Paul
9. Parish Church of the Assumption of Our Lady
10. Parish Church of St. Catherine of Alexandria
11. Minor Basilica of Our Lady of Charity
12. Cathedral of Our Lady of the Atonement
13. Minor Basilica of Our Lady of the Rosary
14. Parish Church of St. James the Great
15. Parish Church of St. James the Great
16. Parish Church of St. William of Aquitaine (San Guillermo de Aquitania)
17. Parish Church of Our Lady of Mt. Carmel
18. Parish Church of the Holy Sacrifice
19. Cathedral-Basilica of the Immaculate Conception of Our Lady
20. San Agustin Church/ Archdiocesan Shrine of Our Lady of Correa
21. Minor Basilica of San Sebastian
22. Minor Basilica of the Black Nazarene (Parish Church of St. John the Baptist)
23. National Shrine of Our Lady of Perpetual Help
24. Parish Church of St. Joseph
25. Parish Church of St. Ildefonse of Toledo

26. Parish Church of the Assumption of Our Lady

27. Parish Church of St. Peter Alcantara

28. Parish Church of St. Gregory the Great

29. Minor Basilica of St. Martin of Tours

30. Minor Basilica of St. Michael the Archangel

31. Parish Church of the Purification of Our Lady (Nuestra Señora de Candelaria)

32. Cathedral of St. John the Evangelist

33. Parish Church of Our Lady of the Gate (Nuestra Señora de la Portería)

34. Parish Church of St. Joseph

35. Parish Church of St. Ignatius of Loyola

36. Parish Church of the Immaculate Conception of Our Lady

37. Parish Church of St. Joseph

38. Minor Basilica of the Holy Child (Santo Niño)

39. Parish Church of the Patronage of Mary (Patrocinio de Maria)

40. Parish Church of the Immaculate Conception of Our Lady

41. Parish Church of the Immaculate Conception of Our Lady

42. Parish Church of St. Augustine of Hippo

43. Parish Church of St. Isidore the Farmer

44. Parish Church of St. Joseph the Worker

45. Parish Church of St. Thomas of Villanova (Santo Tomas de Villanueva)

46. Parish Church of St. John of Nepomuk (San Juan Nepomuceno)

47. Parish Church of St. Mónica

48. Cathedral of St. Joseph

49. Parish Church of St. John the Baptist

50. Parish Church of the Savior of the World (El Salvador del Mundo)

GLOSSARY

Sources of some words are identified as Fil. (Filipino) or Sp. (Spanish).

adobe (Sp.). volcanic tuff, a rock; distinct from the blocks of mud and hay used in America.

apse. the end or "head" of the nave of a church.

atrium. open court in front of a church.

baptistry. space or chapel where persons are baptized into the Christian faith.

baroque. an artistic style characterized by exuberant decoration and motion.

bay. a vertical division of a building, usually marked off by pilasters.

buttress. a mass of masonry erected to support a wall.

C-scroll. a decorative "C" form with both ends rolled like scrolls.

capiz (Hispanized Fil.). thin translucent clams used for windowpanes.

convento (Sp.). the priest's residence; parish house or rectory.

coralstone. rock quarried from coralline sea beds or mountainsides.

Doric. a classical style from Greece and Rome, characterized by a fluted column supporting a frieze of triglyphs alternating with metopes.

frontal. ornamental panel for the front of an altar.

Gothic. an artistic style popularly recognized by its pointed arches, which sprout spiny crockets.

molave (Hispanized Fil.). a hardwood extensively used due to its durability.

nave. the main longitudinal body of a church.

neoclassic. a revival of an artistic style inspired by Greek and Roman buildings, more architectural than sculptural.

newel post. the principal post at either end of a stairway.

palitada (Fil., from Sp. *paletada*). lime plaster applied over a masonry wall for esthetic and protective purposes.

pediment. the upper part of a façade or portico, usually triangular in shape.

pilaster. a rectangular pillar projecting only slightly from a wall.

pulpit. elevated construction, usually attached to a wall, where the priest delivers his homily.

retablo (Sp.). the altarpiece behind the altar table, usually of elaborate design, with niches for images of saints.

rococo. a decorative style characterized by irregular, swirling forms derived from shells, rocks, and foliage.

rubblework. masonry construction using pebbles and rough stone.

S-scroll. a decorative "S" form with both ends rolled like scrolls.

sanctuary. the most sacred space at the head of the church, where mass is celebrated.

tabique pampango (Hispanized Fil.). a light, thin wall of interwoven slats of bamboo or wood, and plastered over with lime.

transept. the "arms" or crossing of a church.

vault. an arched ceiling.

volute. a spiral scroll.

ACKNOWLEDGEMENTS

The Author, Illustrator, and Publishers would like to thank the following for their support and generous contributions for the publication of this book:

Agencia Española de Cooperación Internacional para el Desarrollo, Spain
American Field Service Scholarships, USA
Ateneo de Manila University
Ayala Museum, Philippines
Catholic Bishops' Conference of the Philippines (CBCP)
Cultural Center of the Philippines, Philippines
Department of Foreign Affairs (Philippines), Office of Strategic Communications and Research - Cultural Diplomacy Division
Dominic Velasco
Felice Prudente Sta. Maria
Filipinas Heritage Library, Philippines
Fr. Milan Ted Torralba
Franciscan Sisters of the Immaculate Conception (SFIC), Philippines
Holy Angel University (Angeles City, Philippines)
Honorable Governor Daniel R. Fernando (Provincial Government of Bulacan)
Instituto Cervantes, Manila, Philippines
International Council on Monuments and Sites (ICOMOS), Philippine Chapter
Intramuros Administration, Philippines
Jocelyn Quesada
Lito Sy
López Memorial Museum & Library, Philippines
Mariel Ylagan Garcia
Museo Ilocos Norte (Laoag, Ilocos Norte, Philippines)
National Commission for Culture and the Arts, Philippines
Philippine Madrigal Singers
Philippine National Bank
Philippine National Historical Society
Sr. Alphonse Casambre, SFIC
Sr. Natividad Parin, SFIC
Sr. Severina Aquino, SFIC
The University of Santo Tomas, the Pontifical, Royal, and Catholic University of the Philippines
University of San Carlos (Cebu City, Philippines)
University of the Philippines
Warlito A. Domingo

--At sa mga may pinagdadalubhasaan, pinag-aabalahan at pinag-iingatan napamana ng malakihang bayan, Mabuhay po kayong lahat!

(And to all of you who pursue the specialized study, care and protection of the heritage of the greater nation, more life!)

This book would not have been possible without each and every one of you. We thank you from the bottom of our hearts.

Praying hands of San Pedro de Alcantara
Parish Church of St. Ildefonse of Toledo, Tanay, Rizal

ABOUT THE AUTHOR AND ILLUSTRATOR

REGALADO TROTA JOSÉ

Regalado Trota José has contributed scholarly books and articles towards the study and protection of the cultural heritage of the Philippines since the 1980s. He obtained his A.B. in Anthropology (1978) and M.A. in Philippine Studies (Art History, 1991) from the University of the Philippines. His *Simbahan: Church Art in Colonial Philippines 1565-1898* won the National Book Award in the Art Category in 1992.

José received the Cultural Center of the Philippines Centennial Award for the Arts in 1999. He was the youngest awardee among "100 Outstanding Filipinos who have helped build the Filipino nation through art and culture during the last 100 years."

He collaborates with institutions such as the Catholic Bishops' Conference of the Philippines (C.B.C.P.), and the National Commission for Culture and Arts (N.C.C.A.), where he was former commissioner for Cultural Heritage. He sang and traveled with the Philippine Madrigal Singers, too.

José teaches at the Cultural Heritage Studies Program of the University of Santo Tomas, where he has been the Archivist since 2010.

ALLAN JAY QUESADA

Allan Jay Quesada is a photographer, a painter and an architect. He has the eye, the hand and the technical background that produced the inspired illustrations of Simbahán.

The kilometric list of awards for this works from his pre-teen years through his adolescence and school years of secondary and tertiary levels speaks volumes about the rapid progression and maturation of his art. This list consistently stretched up to his current professional status.

He won the Grand Prize of the Churches of the North Photo Competition in 2018 here. He won the Grand Prize in May 2019 in Madrid, Spain at the Climate Tracker and WHO's Climate Change and Health Photo Competition.

He started watercolor painting at 5 years of age. His works are mostly landscapes, urban scenes and heritage structures. He looks up to Alvaro Castagnet and Joseph Zbukvic, his watercolor idols.

Allan gives free painting and rendering seminars in his alma mater, Pamantasan ng Lungsod ng Maynila (P.L.M.). His YouTube Channel is "Watercolors by Allan Jay Quesada". He shares regular tutorials there.

He belongs to the International Watercolor Society of the Philippines. He has been a member of the United Architects of the Philippines – Manila Maharlika Chapter since 2011.